Master AI for Beginners

By

CHARLIE HANSEN

Develop Artificial Intelligence Basics, Understand Machine Learning, and Unlock the Power of Automation for Business Productivity and Everyday Life

TABLE OF CONTENTS

TABLE OF CONTENTS	**2**
INTRODUCTION	**6**
CHAPTER 1	**8**
FOUNDATIONS OF ARTIFICIAL INTELLIGENCE	**8**
WHAT IS ARTIFICIAL INTELLIGENCE?	8
REFLECTION EXERCISE	10
KEY TERMINOLOGIES SIMPLIFIED	10
INTERACTIVE ELEMENT: QUICK QUIZ	11
THE EVOLUTION OF AI AND ITS CURRENT ROLE	12
AI VS. MACHINE LEARNING: UNDERSTANDING THE DIFFERENCES	14
DEBUNKING MYTHS: AI IN EVERYDAY LANGUAGE	16
CHAPTER 2	**18**
DIVING INTO MACHINE LEARNING	**18**
MACHINE LEARNING 101: AN OVERVIEW	18
REFLECTION SECTION: DATA IN YOUR LIFE	20
SUPERVISED VS. UNSUPERVISED LEARNING	20
DECISION TREES AND THEIR BUSINESS APPLICATIONS	22
CASE STUDY: DECISION TREES IN ACTION	23
INTRODUCTION TO NEURAL NETWORKS	23
COMMON PITFALLS IN MACHINE LEARNING: WHAT TO AVOID	25
CHAPTER 3	**27**
PRACTICAL AI APPLICATIONS IN BUSINESS	**27**

AI IN MARKETING: PERSONALIZATION AND ANALYTICS	27
INTERACTIVE ELEMENT: REFLECTION SECTION	29
AUTOMATING CUSTOMER SERVICE WITH AI	30
ENHANCING PRODUCTIVITY IN OPERATIONS THROUGH AI	33
VISUAL ELEMENT: INFOGRAPHIC	34
FINANCIAL FORECASTING WITH AI TOOLS	35
BUILDING AN AI-DRIVEN BUSINESS STRATEGY	37

CHAPTER 4   39

EVERYDAY LIFE WITH AI	**39**
SMART HOMES: AI-POWERED CONVENIENCES	39
INTERACTIVE ELEMENT: REFLECTION SECTION	41
HEALTH AND WELLNESS: AI AS A PERSONAL ASSISTANT	41
INTERACTIVE ELEMENT: REFLECTION SECTION	44
AI IN EDUCATION: PERSONALISED LEARNING PATHS	44
VISUAL ELEMENT: INFOGRAPHIC	46
TRAVEL PLANNING SIMPLIFIED WITH AI TOOLS	47
VISUAL ELEMENT: INFOGRAPHIC	48
AI IN ENTERTAINMENT: TAILORING YOUR EXPERIENCE	49

CHAPTER 5   52

VISUALIZING AI CONCEPTS	**52**
VISUALIZING DATA: THE ROLE OF AI IN BUSINESS INTELLIGENCE	52
VISUAL ELEMENT: INTERACTIVE EXERCISE	53
INFOGRAPHICS: SIMPLIFYING AI TRENDS AND PREDICTIONS	54
REFLECTION SECTION: CREATE YOUR OWN INFOGRAPHIC	56
MAKE A DIFFERENCE WITH YOUR REVIEW	56

CHAPTER 6   58

ETHICAL AI AND ITS IMPLICATIONS	**58**
PRIVACY CONCERNS IN AI: WHAT YOU NEED TO KNOW	58
REFLECTION EXERCISE: BALANCING PRIVACY AND INNOVATION	59
ALGORITHMIC BIAS: IDENTIFYING AND MITIGATING RISKS	60
REFLECTION SECTION: BIAS IN EVERYDAY ALGORITHMS	62
RESPONSIBLE AI: PRINCIPLES AND PRACTICES	62
INTERACTIVE ELEMENT: CASE STUDY REFLECTION	64
ETHICAL DILEMMAS IN AI: REAL-WORLD CASE STUDIES	65
FUTURE-PROOFING ETHICS IN AI DEVELOPMENT	66

CHAPTER 7   69

FUTURE TRENDS AND EMERGING TECHNOLOGIES	**69**
AI AND THE INTERNET OF THINGS (IOT): A CONNECTED FUTURE	69
REFLECTION SECTION	71
CLOUD COMPUTING AND AI: A SYNERGISTIC RELATIONSHIP	72
THE RISE OF AI IN CYBERSECURITY	74
AI IN AUTONOMOUS VEHICLES: STEERING TOWARDS THE FUTURE	77
REFLECTION SECTION	79
PREDICTING AI'S NEXT BIG TRENDS	80

CHAPTER 8   83

EMPOWERING CAREERS WITH AI	**83**
UPSKILLING WITH AI: CAREER ADVANCEMENT STRATEGIES	83
INTERACTIVE ELEMENT: REFLECTION SECTION	85
NAVIGATING AI TOOLS FOR PROFESSIONAL GROWTH	85
INTERACTIVE ELEMENT: CASE STUDY	87
AI CERTIFICATION AND LEARNING RESOURCES	87
VISUAL ELEMENT: RESOURCE LIST	89
COMMUNICATING AI CONCEPTS TO NON-TECHNICAL TEAMS	89
TEXTUAL ELEMENT: REFLECTION SECTION	90
BUILDING AN AI-READY RESUME	91

Visual Element: Checklist 92

CHAPTER 9 — 93

Overcoming Challenges in AI Learning — 93
Overcoming the Intimidation Factor: AI-Made Accessible — 93
Reflection Section: Your AI Path Forward — 94
Avoiding Information Overload: Curating Your AI Learning Path — 95
Engaging with AI Communities: Learning Together — 96
Staying Updated: Tools and Resources for Continuous Learning — 97
Embracing Mistakes: Learning and Growing with AI — 98

CHAPTER 10 — 100

Realizing the Potential of AI — 100
Case Studies: AI Success Stories Across Industries — 100
Interactive Element: Reflecting on AI's Impact — 104
The Human-AI Collaboration: Enhancing Creativity and Innovation — 105
Envisioning the Future: Your Role in the AI Revolution — 109

CONCLUSION — 112

Keeping the Knowledge Alive — 113

REFERENCES — 115

Introduction

Consider this: A recent study found that 77% of people use an AI-powered service daily without realizing it. Whether it's the recommendation for your next movie or the intelligent assistant scheduling your meetings, AI is subtly weaving itself into the fabric of our lives. Yet, despite its growing presence, artificial intelligence remains a mystery to many. This book aims to change that.

My journey with AI began not in a lab but in the bustling office of a mid-sized company. I watched as seasoned professionals struggled to understand how AI could fit into their daily routines. Then, I realized that the barrier was not the complexity of AI itself but how it was explained. This realization ignited my passion for making AI accessible to non-technical professionals and students. I wanted to demystify AI and show that it is not the exclusive domain of tech experts.

The purpose of this book is straightforward. It is an easy-to-read guide designed to simplify the basics of AI. I aim to show you how AI can enhance both business productivity and everyday life. Whether you're a manager looking to optimize operations or a student curious about the future of work, this book is for you. We will explore practical applications that you can implement immediately.

You might wonder if this book is right for you. The answer is yes if you're a non-technical professional or a student eager to grasp AI's potential. This book is beneficial because it breaks down complex ideas into manageable pieces. You'll learn how AI can make your tasks easier and your processes more efficient.

Here's how the book is structured: We begin with the basics, exploring what AI is and how it works. Each chapter builds on the previous one, gradually introducing more advanced concepts. We'll cover machine learning, automation, and the impact of AI on different industries. Real-life examples and case studies will show how these concepts apply in various contexts. By the end, you'll have a roadmap for integrating AI into your life.

It's important to address common misconceptions about AI. Many believe AI is too complex or that it will replace human jobs. Others think it's only for tech giants. This book will clarify these misunderstandings. AI is accessible and can benefit everyone, regardless of their technical background.

We'll focus a lot on real-life implications. Each concept comes with examples that demonstrate how AI is already changing industries. You'll see how businesses streamline operations and how individuals boost productivity. These insights will help you apply what you learn right away.

I encourage you to approach this journey with curiosity. AI is a field ripe with possibilities. Maintaining an open mind will enhance your learning experience. Engage with the content actively and explore AI's potential.

By the end of this book, you can expect a solid understanding of AI fundamentals. You'll have actionable strategies to leverage AI in your personal and professional life. This knowledge will set you on a path to becoming more productive and efficient.

I invite you to join me on this educational journey. Together, we'll explore the fascinating world of AI, uncover its mysteries, and learn how it can transform our lives. Welcome aboard. Let's get started.

Chapter 1

Foundations of Artificial Intelligence

You're seated in a quaint café, the aroma of freshly brewed coffee enveloping you as a conversation about artificial intelligence (AI) catches your attention. No longer just industry chatter, AI has become a transformative force, shaping large-scale industries and the smallest nuances of daily life. From recommending your next streaming binge to driving breakthroughs in medical diagnostics, its pervasive presence raises essential questions: What exactly is AI? How does it operate? And, as a citizen of the digital age, why is it crucial to understand this technology?

This chapter unpacks these complexities, exploring the foundational elements of artificial intelligence.

What is Artificial Intelligence?

pattern recognition. They power applications like image and speech recognition. Every time you use voice commands on your phone or encounter facial recognition in security systems and social media, you're engaging with a neural network that maps features and refines responses based on learned patterns.

Now, enter the world of "deep learning." If neural networks resemble brain activity, deep learning is akin to a symphony orchestra—layers working in harmony, with each refining data interpretations. This enables tasks like filtering spam emails with remarkable precision or helping autonomous vehicles navigate complex traffic scenarios and sudden road changes.

Understanding "data mining" further illuminates these concepts. Much like panning for gold, data mining extracts valuable insights from massive datasets. In marketing, it deciphers consumer behaviors to craft personalised advertisements. Ever noticed how social media ads seem tailored to your interests? That's data mining in action, continuously evolving based on user interactions.

Another crucial term is "natural language processing" (NLP), which enables machines to understand and respond to human language. Picture calling customer service and conversing with an AI that interprets your questions and provides relevant solutions. NLP also powers real-time translation, breaking down global communication barriers and transforming business interactions.

To put it into perspective, neural networks function like brain neurons, learning and improving over time—much like your initial struggles when learning to ride a bike. Machine learning follows this principle, continuously refining performance through new data and experiences.

Mastering these terms isn't just about expanding vocabulary—it's about engaging in AI discussions with confidence. Whether evaluating AI tools or contributing to workplace innovation, understanding concepts like deep learning or NLP equips you to assess technology critically. Imagine discussing AI-driven operational efficiency: recognizing how neural networks predict customer trends or how NLP enhances client interactions enables you to provide informed, strategic insights.

Interactive Element: Quick Quiz

1. How can an algorithm best be described?
2. What parallels exist between neural networks and the human brain?
3. In what way does deep learning contribute to spam detection?

Reflect on these questions as you encounter AI technologies in your daily life. Developing familiarity with these concepts builds confidence, allowing you to navigate the evolving AI landscape with ease.

By understanding these terminologies, you become better equipped to engage with AI on multiple levels. Whether discussing emerging AI tools in the workplace or recognizing how technology enhances everyday experiences, this knowledge opens the door to new opportunities and deeper insights.

The Evolution of AI and Its Current Role

The saga of AI development resembles a narrative punctuated with twists, setbacks, and victories, mirroring a modern epic. The journey commences with the 1956 Dartmouth Conference, the cradle of AI as an academic discipline. Visionaries at this convergence foresaw machines executing tasks usually reserved for the human intellect. By the 1970s, expert systems emerged, emulating human decision-making processes and validating the notion of machine cognition. Yet, the trajectory wasn't continuous; "AI winters" marked periods of halted momentum due to waning interest and fiscal constraints. But like a cyclical rebirth, AI perpetually emerged stronger, spurred by advancements in computational capacity and algorithmic ingenuity.

In contemporary society, AI seamlessly integrates into everyday instances and broader institutional infrastructures. Consider smart home devices integral to modern domestic life—adjusting room temperatures via smart thermostats or brewing coffee at optimally programmed schedules. These devices exemplify how AI delivers convenience and efficiency. On a broader scale, AI-powered algorithms elegantly curate personalised content feeds on social media, subtly influencing digital consumption patterns without users being conscious of their actions. AI's utility extends to public domains, optimizing urban traffic flows in smart cities, thus reducing carbon footprints or predicting meteorological trends to bolster disaster preparedness.

Looking toward the future, AI's potential seems unbounded, catalysing profound innovations. Quantum computing is a frontier poised to revolutionize AI, exponentially augmenting processing power. Envision AI systems adept at resolving challenges that currently elude the capacity of the world's fastest supercomputers. Such progression could revolutionize the pharmaceutical sector, accelerating drug discovery and precipitating timely medical advancements. Equally transformative are autonomous systems, spanning self-driving vehicles maneuvering urban landscapes to drones managing doorstep deliveries. These anticipated advancements underscore AI's formidable potential to redefine societal contours. Smart agriculture, utilizing AI to optimize irrigation and pest control, highlights another horizon for sustainable development.

AI's impact on the workforce invigorates nuanced dialogue around future employment landscapes. As AI assumes routine tasks like data entry or customer service inquiries, human talent is liberated to engage in more intricate, innovative pursuits. This evolution is not about job annihilation but about transitioning workplace functions. While some roles may wane, fresh avenues arise in new sectors like AI ethics or data interpretation, where human insight remains crucial. For instance, contemplate the ascent of data scientists distilling AI-derived insights or ethicists ensuring AI technologies adhere to ethical benchmarks.

AI's pervasive influence shifts employer preferences for skill sets, emphasizing critical thinking, adaptability, and technical proficiency. As industries embrace AI integration, continuous learning emerges as essential. Employees must be willing to upskill and reskill, ensuring competitiveness in a dynamically evolving job market. This transition presents both challenges and opportunities as organizations and individuals navigate AI integration.

Amidst this rapid evolution, cultivating curiosity and adaptability is paramount. Whether preparing for prospective careers or enhancing existing professional practices, understanding AI's trajectory equips individuals to accommodate transformative shifts pragmatically. As your exploration of this book deepens, perceive AI not solely as a technological premium but as a catalyst driving innovation and growth across multidimensional life spectrums. Engaging with AI compels us to rethink the interplay between technology and society, fostering a culture of innovation that propels humanity forward.

AI vs. Machine Learning: Understanding the Differences

Artificial intelligence is a broad umbrella encompassing various technologies designed to replicate human-like cognition. Under this umbrella, machine learning serves as a specialized mechanism that enables systems to learn autonomously from data and improve performance without explicit programming. It focuses on developing algorithms that adapt based on new inputs, much like refining culinary skills through experimentation.

Machine learning thrives on data, refining its predictive accuracy as more information becomes available. This process mirrors how children learn to identify animals by seeing a variety of pictures. The continuous evolution of machine learning allows for nuanced improvements and adaptive decision-making.

While AI represents the overarching goal of creating intelligent machines, machine learning is a key pathway within that vision. AI includes a wide range of techniques, from rule-based systems to natural language processing, whereas machine learning specifically extracts patterns from data. For example, AI powers autonomous vehicles through sensors and decision-making algorithms, while machine learning fine-tunes these systems to adapt to new environments, such as adjusting driving behaviors for inclement weather.

The practical applications of AI highlight its transformative potential in automating complex workflows and enhancing strategic decision-making. Consider how an autonomous vehicle relies on AI for situational awareness and context-specific decisions. Machine learning builds upon this by continuously improving driving performance through experiential learning, adapting to different traffic patterns and weather conditions. Similarly, AI enables precision automation in manufacturing, while machine learning optimizes supply chains by predicting demand fluctuations.

Machine learning excels in predictive analytics, from forecasting sales trends to detecting fraudulent transactions. By analysing historical datasets, machine learning models provide accurate future projections, allowing businesses to make data-driven strategic decisions. In healthcare, these models predict patient readmissions, helping hospitals plan treatments and allocate resources efficiently.

Despite its widespread impact, misconceptions often cloud our understanding of AI and machine learning. One common misconception is that AI is a standalone entity, rather than a network of interdependent technologies. Another is the belief that machine learning functions independently of large datasets. Just as musicians require practice to perfect their craft, machine learning depends on extensive, high-quality data to generate reliable insights. Without sufficient data, its predictions lack accuracy.

Machine learning's effectiveness hinges on robust datasets. Imagine trying to predict climate patterns based on limited observations—such an approach would yield unreliable results. Similarly, machine learning requires vast amounts of data to recognize patterns accurately, emphasizing the importance of data integrity.

Recognizing the distinctions between AI and machine learning fosters a deeper understanding of their roles in modern technology. Rather than viewing them as separate, it is essential to see their symbiotic relationship. AI represents the vision of intelligent machines, while machine learning powers that vision through continuous adaptation. Together, they drive breakthroughs across various fields, from enhancing medical diagnostics to improving financial risk management.

AI's influence extends into everyday life, automating tasks and curating personalised experiences. Whether through tailored movie recommendations or automated customer service interactions, AI's presence is undeniable. Machine learning enhances these experiences by analysing user preferences to deliver seamless, customized solutions.

Understanding the difference between AI and machine learning provides a foundation for meaningful discussions about technology's role in society. This knowledge helps assess AI's transformative potential across industries. As you explore this topic further, keep in mind the ever-evolving relationship between human ambition and technological advancement. The conversation around AI's future will only continue to grow, shaping the world in unprecedented ways.

Debunking Myths: AI in Everyday Language

AI is often the subject of exaggerated portrayals and dystopian myths, fueling fears about its role in society. Imagine gripping narratives where AI eclipses human roles, rendering us obsolete. While these scenarios are compelling, they are not rooted in reality. AI is not designed to replace humanity; rather, it enhances our capabilities. It serves as an invaluable tool that amplifies human efficiency rather than eliminating human functions. For instance, AI's ability to rapidly analyse data assists doctors in refining diagnostic accuracy, but it does not replace their expertise. This synergy between human intellect and machine precision exemplifies AI's true potential.

One of the most widespread fears is that AI will consume all jobs, leaving the workforce obsolete. The reality is far more nuanced. While AI does automate certain tasks, it also generates new opportunities. History provides a precedent—the Industrial Revolution once sparked fears of mass unemployment, yet it ultimately gave rise to new industries and professions. Similarly, AI today relieves humans of repetitive tasks, allowing them to focus on creativity, strategy, and problem-solving. In finance, for example, AI efficiently handles data analysis, freeing professionals to prioritize client relationships and high-level decision-making. This transition requires adaptation but also paves the way for emerging career paths.

Addressing these misconceptions requires accurate information. AI optimizes human potential by handling routine tasks, allowing us to engage in complex, high-value work. Ethical frameworks guide AI development to ensure it aligns with human values and safety standards. Organizations like UNESCO advocate for transparent and accountable AI systems, helping to prevent misuse and promote AI's role in advancing human well-being.

Rather than an existential threat, AI should be viewed as an empowering assistant. Just as a calculator simplifies arithmetic, AI enhances complex processes. Similar to how washing machines and dishwashers revolutionized domestic labor, AI is transforming modern workflows, increasing productivity and efficiency. By automating time-consuming tasks, AI enables individuals and businesses to achieve more than ever before.

A well-informed perspective on AI fosters critical thinking, dispelling fear and misinformation. Recognizing AI's constructive role in everyday life highlights its value in improving efficiency and decision-making. From smart home devices to personalised shopping experiences, AI's benefits are already integrated into daily routines. By understanding its real-world applications, we move beyond myths and cultivate a rational, balanced perspective on AI's potential.

Ethical considerations remain at the forefront of AI's development. Prioritizing fairness, transparency, and privacy ensures that AI systems foster trust and responsible integration into society. The societal impact of AI must be carefully guided to uphold human-centered values, shaping a future where technology serves humanity rather than disrupting it.

As AI continues to evolve, approaching it with curiosity and openness allows us to embrace its transformative potential while maintaining ethical vigilance. By actively engaging in discussions about AI's role, we can help shape its future responsibly, balancing innovation with accountability.

In conclusion, despite dystopian myths, the reality of AI is far more optimistic. Rather than overshadowing humanity, AI serves as a powerful tool that augments human abilities without replacing them. By dispelling misconceptions and embracing AI's true potential, we can approach technological advancements with confidence and ethical mindfulness. As we navigate this digital era, AI stands not as a threat but as a catalyst for unprecedented innovation and possibilities.

Chapter 2

Diving into Machine Learning

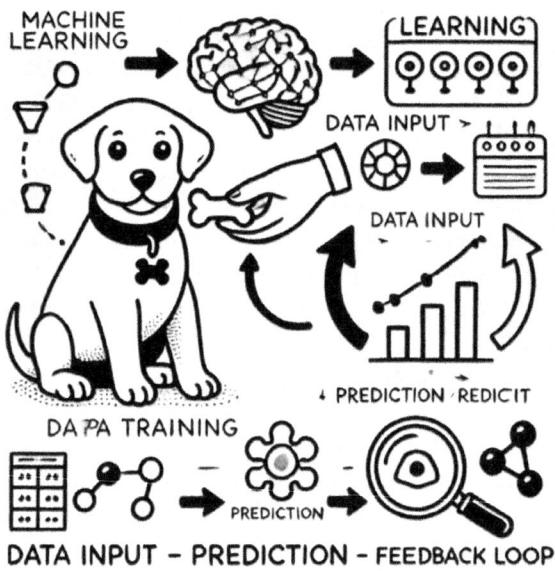

Machine Learning 101: An Overview

Imagine a setting where visiting your favorite coffee shop means the barista knows you so well that your cappuccino is ready and waiting just as you arrive at the counter. Now, picture a computer doing something similar—learning patterns and making data-based decisions. That's the essence of machine learning. This technology enables computers to learn, understand, and adapt autonomously by analysing vast amounts of data. Unlike traditional programming, which explicitly dictates every action a computer must perform, machine learning takes a more autonomous approach, allowing systems to uncover insights without constant human intervention. This ability lets machines recognize subtle patterns, predict outcomes, and even recommend actions—much like a barista anticipating your order before you even ask.

At its core, machine learning transforms data into meaningful pattern recognition. It enables systems to learn autonomously, perceive trends, and make informed decisions with minimal human input. Imagine training a puppy: you reward it with treats (data) when it responds correctly, gradually teaching it to sit or stay. This mirrors predictive modeling, a key aspect of machine learning. By analysing historical data, machine learning models can predict future trends, helping businesses anticipate sales forecasts or understand consumer behavior.

The machine learning process follows an iterative cycle. It begins with data collection, where relevant information is gathered for the model to learn from. However, raw data often needs preprocessing—like tidying a cluttered room to find valuable items. Data cleansing removes inconsistencies and noise, preparing the dataset for training. During model training, the system identifies patterns and makes predictions. The model is then evaluated for performance, refined if necessary, and finally deployed. Once in operation, it undergoes continuous monitoring to ensure optimal accuracy and effectiveness.

Machine learning is revolutionizing industries. In healthcare, it enhances diagnostics by analysing medical images and identifying diseases with remarkable precision. For instance, algorithms assist radiologists by highlighting areas in scans that may require further examination, improving diagnostic efficiency and reducing human error. In marketing, machine learning personalises customer interactions by analysing consumer data to tailor content and advertisements to individual preferences. These strategies significantly boost engagement and conversion rates, optimizing marketing efforts.

Despite its growing impact, machine learning is often misunderstood. A common misconception is that it's reserved for tech experts with extensive coding skills. While technical knowledge is helpful, machine learning is becoming increasingly accessible. User-friendly platforms allow non-experts to explore machine learning applications without deep programming expertise. Additionally, domain knowledge often outweighs coding proficiency—understanding an industry improves data selection and result interpretation.

Another myth suggests that machine learning is too complex for the average person. While some processes can be intricate, the fundamental idea is simple: using data to make informed decisions. Learning machine learning is like mastering any skill—you start with the basics and refine your understanding through practice and experience.

Reflection Section: Data in Your Life

Reflect on your daily routine and consider where you encounter data-driven technologies. How do they enhance your life? Machine learning plays a crucial role in optimizing these experiences. Think of streaming services that use algorithms to recommend shows based on your viewing history or navigation apps that analyse traffic patterns to suggest the fastest routes. By reflecting on these interactions, you can recognize the subtle yet powerful ways machine learning refines and revolutionizes everyday experiences.

By dispelling myths and highlighting real-world applications, we aim to make machine learning more accessible to everyone. It's about enhancing human capabilities in ways we might not have anticipated. As you explore machine learning further, keep an open mind about its potential to transform industries and improve life on a broader scale.

Supervised vs. Unsupervised Learning

Imagine training a dog to sit on command. You give it a treat every time it sits when you say "sit." This demonstration closely mirrors supervised learning. In supervised learning, models train with labeled datasets, where each input is tied to an output. It's akin to furnishing an instructional manual for the computer. You provide extensive examples, offering the correct answer each time, allowing the model to predict independently and accurately. A practical example is spam detection. Emails categorized as "spam" or "not spam" help systems discern patterns, filtering junk mail effectively. Another application is predicting house prices; historically, inputs like the number of bedrooms, location, and size have allowed models to estimate property values with impressive accuracy.

Now, let's explore unsupervised learning. This is akin to exploration without a map, seeking undiscovered patterns in data without preassigned labels. This method doesn't rely on predefined answers but proactively seeks structures or groupings within a dataset. Clustering is fundamental here and is often used in customer segmentation. Businesses cluster customers based on behaviors, refining marketing strategies for targeted efforts. Anomaly detection, such as identifying fraudulent transactions, uses unsupervised learning to recognize outliers as potential fraud, distinguishing deviations from "normal."

Both methods have unique applications, displaying individual strengths. Supervised learning shines in areas demanding accuracy, such as image recognition, where systems trained with labeled images identify objects or scenes precisely—it's like teaching children animal names through labeled picture books. Conversely, unsupervised learning excels in exploratory scenarios. Recommendation systems are a prime example. Analysing user behavior without clear labels, these systems offer product suggestions tailored to preferences, enhancing user experience.

Each approach's strengths and limitations make them suitable for varied tasks. Supervised learning is impactful with extensive labeled data, functioning like a clear guide. Yet, acquiring datasets can be time-consuming. Moreover, supervised models might struggle with new data types they haven't been trained on. Unsupervised learning transcends the need for labeled data, offering flexibility across varying scenarios. It's great for uncovering unknown dataset structures. However, result interpretation is challenging without predetermined categories or labels, occasionally making it less intuitive than supervised models.

Understanding these approaches provides a foundation for machine learning tasks. Supervised learning offers precision through clear guidelines, while unsupervised learning encourages exploration and innovation by delving into uncharted data analysis territories. Recognizing when to employ each method and embracing its benefits and limitations equips you to unleash machine learning's full potential in real-world applications.

Decision Trees and Their Business Applications

Envision decision trees as methodical flowcharts. They're tree-structured models that divide data into branches, guiding decisions based on various criteria. Each node signifies a decision point, leading to branches that culminate in a result. This layout makes decision trees remarkably intuitive. Imagine deciding whether to take an umbrella. You start with, "Is it cloudy?" If yes, the next node asks, "Do you have weather alerts?" Progressing through these steps leads to a final decision—to carry the umbrella or not. In machine learning, decision trees excel in both classification and regression tasks, categorizing items or predicting values and enhancing diverse applications.

In business, decision trees resemble versatile Swiss Army knives. Consider the telecom industry, where predicting customer churn is vital. Decision trees scrutinize customer behavior, identifying those likely to switch providers. By recognizing patterns, companies can effectively strategize on customer retention. In the financial sector, decision trees excel in risk assessment. They evaluate factors like credit scores and debts to estimate loan default probabilities, empowering well-judged lending decisions that balance risk and opportunity.

Decision trees are notable for their visual clarity. They make intricate decision paths comprehensible even for non-experts, akin to explaining reasoning through visuals. A decision tree elucidates complexity with clarity. They also require no data normalization, eliminating the need to harmonize variable scales. This simplicity reduces preprocessing time, enhancing user-friendliness.

However, decision trees also have drawbacks. Overfitting, where models become excessively tailored to training data, hampers their ability to generalize to new data. It's similar to memorizing test answers rather than understanding concepts—practical for a test but ineffective elsewhere. Additionally, data imbalance can bias trees, skewing outcomes.

Techniques like pruning—removing unnecessary branches to prevent overfitting—help address these challenges. This is similar to editing an essay by removing redundancy to improve clarity. Ensemble methods like Random Forests or Gradient Boosting bolster performance by unifying multiple trees into one model, reducing variance and increasing accuracy.

Despite these challenges, decision trees remain popular due to their interpretability and simplicity. They offer transparent decision-making insights, which are invaluable for businesses seeking model accountability. Their flexibility with both categorical and numerical data broadens their industry applications.

Case Study: Decision Trees in Action

Explore how a retail company leveraged decision trees to optimize inventory management and reduce waste. By analysing sales patterns and customer preferences, the company refined its stock levels, improving customer satisfaction while enhancing efficiency and profitability.

Through real-world examples, decision trees demonstrate their potential to drive success by providing actionable insights and enabling data-driven decision-making. They combine simplicity with effectiveness, making them an appealing choice for organizations seeking practical solutions without sacrificing interpretability. If you're exploring machine learning, consider decision trees—they may uncover new opportunities and valuable insights in your field.

Introduction to Neural Networks

Imagine your brain's neurons firing as you read this sentence, intricately interlinked to process information. Computing's neural networks emulate this by structuring layers of interconnected nodes—artificial neurons. These layers process inputs, passing outcomes to subsequent layers until reaching a conclusion. Neural networks learn and adapt, making them essential to deep learning. The multiple layers in deep learning enable the recognition of complex patterns, much like identifying faces in a crowd or understanding the nuances of language.

Neural network architectures vary, each suited to distinct tasks and offering remarkable versatility. Convolutional Neural Networks (CNNs) excel in image processing, analysing visuals by breaking images into smaller regions and identifying patterns such as edges. This capability has driven advancements in medical imaging and autonomous vehicles, where precise image interpretation is crucial. Meanwhile, Recurrent Neural Networks (RNNs) handle sequential data effectively, making them ideal for time-series forecasting and language translation. RNNs retain information from previous steps, which is vital for tasks that require context and continuity.

The practical applications of neural networks span various industries, showcasing their adaptability. In speech recognition, they power virtual assistants like Siri and Alexa, enabling them to understand spoken requests by recognizing sound patterns. Text prediction is another familiar application—predictive keyboards analyse keystrokes, suggest words based on usage habits, and streamline communication to enhance user experience.

Despite their potential, implementing neural networks presents challenges. Deep networks require significant computational power and memory, necessitating specialized hardware like GPUs. Additionally, extensive labeled datasets are essential for effective learning, but acquiring and curating high-quality data can be costly and time-consuming, posing a barrier for many organizations.

The complexity of neural networks also raises interpretability concerns. Unlike simpler models, they often function as "black boxes," making it difficult to understand how decisions are made. This lack of transparency can be problematic in critical fields such as healthcare and finance. To address this, techniques like attention mechanisms help highlight influential inputs, improving interpretability.

Another challenge is overfitting, where networks become overly tailored to training data and struggle to generalize to new inputs. Mitigation strategies such as regularization help by reducing reliance on specific nodes, improving flexibility and robustness.

Despite these challenges, neural networks are revolutionizing technology across industries. Their ability to recognize patterns and solve complex problems is reshaping fields once considered beyond the reach of traditional methods. As computational power advances and training techniques evolve, their influence will continue to expand.

Understanding neural networks provides insight into the cutting-edge technologies shaping the digital world. From language processing to image recognition, their applications are vast. Recognizing both their capabilities and limitations enhances our appreciation of their role in driving innovation across personal and professional domains.

Common Pitfalls in Machine Learning: What to Avoid

As we embark on our machine learning journeys, it's easy to fall into common pitfalls that can compromise model effectiveness or lead to misleading outcomes. Two notable challenges are overfitting and underfitting. Overfitting occurs when a model becomes too tailored to training data, including noise, performing well during training but poorly on new data—much like memorizing exam answers without understanding the concepts. Underfitting, on the other hand, happens when a model is too simplistic to capture underlying trends, akin to having too few puzzle pieces to see the full picture. Both scenarios result in skewed predictions and reduced performance.

Neglecting data quality is another major pitfall. Data forms the foundation of machine learning—disorganized or inaccurate data leads to unreliable models, much like building on unstable ground. Ensuring data cleanliness and real-world representation before training provides a strong base for model development.

How can we avoid these pitfalls and improve model performance? Cross-validation is a valuable technique that ensures models perform well across diverse data subsets, not just the training set. This approach is similar to refining a recipe by testing it with different ingredients. Additionally, proper feature selection and engineering play a crucial role—choosing relevant variables, creating new features, and capturing meaningful data patterns. This process is like selecting the best ingredients and preparing them thoughtfully to enhance a dish's flavor.

Domain knowledge is also essential. Understanding the context of a model helps in selecting relevant variables and interpreting results accurately. It's similar to knowing the rules of a game before playing. For instance, predicting stock prices requires insights into market trends and economic factors, enabling the development of precise, tailored models.

Beyond accuracy, interpretability is key, especially in decision-making. Imagine relying on a model to determine the necessity of surgery—you'd want to understand how it arrived at its conclusion. This is where interpretability becomes crucial. Explainable AI techniques make models more transparent and understandable, fostering trust and facilitating troubleshooting. Balancing accuracy with interpretability ensures that stakeholders can comprehend and confidently rely on model-driven decisions.

In conclusion, avoiding common machine learning pitfalls requires vigilance and strategic approaches. Emphasizing data quality, applying cross-validation, leveraging domain expertise, and ensuring interpretability all contribute to building robust, reliable models. Each step strengthens the foundation for machine learning success, leading to insights you can trust.

Next, we explore how AI and machine learning integrate into everyday tasks, simplifying complex processes. As we move forward, stay curious about automation's powerful impact on productivity and daily life.

Chapter 3

Practical AI Applications in Business

AI in Marketing: Personalization and Analytics

Picture this: You're scrolling through your favorite online store, and it feels like the site knows what you need before you do. This isn't magic—it's AI-driven personalization at work. AI has revolutionized marketing by tailoring experiences to individual preferences, making interactions feel personal and engaging. By analysing past interactions, AI algorithms predict which products or services you're likely to be interested in—much like a friendly shopkeeper who remembers your favorite items. This personalised approach increases engagement and conversion rates because it resonates with consumers on a deeper level. When marketing feels relevant, it captures attention and fosters loyalty.

Beyond personalization, AI plays a crucial role in customer journey mapping. By collecting and analysing data from various channels, AI constructs detailed visual representations of customer interactions throughout their engagement with a brand. These insights help businesses identify where potential customers drop off and refine touchpoints to enhance retention.

One of the most impactful applications of AI in marketing is personalised email campaigns. These go beyond generic, one-size-fits-all messages. AI algorithms meticulously analyse user behavior, preferences, and past interactions to craft emails that speak directly to each recipient—like a friend who remembers your birthdays and anniversaries. This targeted approach significantly increases engagement because the emails address specific needs or interests. For example, if you frequently browse a particular category, you might receive an email highlighting new arrivals in that area, enticing you to explore further.

AI-powered A/B testing takes personalised email campaigns a step further. By automatically analysing the effectiveness of different variations—such as subject lines, call-to-action buttons, and content layout—businesses can determine which elements drive the highest engagement. This continuous optimization ensures that marketing strategies remain effective and responsive to consumer preferences.

Dynamic content creation is another way AI personalises marketing efforts. By analysing user behavior in real-time, AI can adjust website content to match individual preferences. Imagine visiting a site that reorganizes itself to showcase products based on your recent searches or browsing history. This tailored experience keeps users engaged by presenting relevant content that captures their interest and encourages deeper exploration. It's akin to walking into a store where every display is curated just for you.

Beyond personalization, AI empowers marketers with predictive analytics. By analysing consumer data, AI forecasts trends and behaviors, enabling businesses to develop proactive strategies. Predictive customer segmentation plays a vital role in this process, grouping customers based on expected behavior and allowing for highly targeted marketing campaigns. This ensures that marketing efforts are focused where they're most likely to yield results.

Predictive analytics also helps businesses anticipate market demand shifts. By identifying emerging patterns, AI can forecast changes in consumer preferences or market conditions. With this insight, businesses can adjust their strategies to stay ahead of competitors. It's like having a crystal ball that reveals future trends, guiding informed decision-making.

AI-powered chatbots are also revolutionizing customer interactions. These virtual assistants provide round-the-clock support, ensuring customers receive immediate responses whenever needed. Imagine a friendly assistant who never sleeps, ready to answer questions, resolve issues, and assist customers in real time. Using natural language processing, chatbots handle FAQs seamlessly, mimicking human conversations and enhancing customer satisfaction by delivering quick, accurate responses. This automation improves efficiency while building trust and reliability with the brand.

Measuring marketing ROI has traditionally been challenging, but AI is changing that. Real-time performance tracking dashboards provide instant insights into campaign effectiveness, allowing marketers to monitor metrics such as click-through rates, engagement levels, and conversions as they unfold. This enables data-driven adjustments on the fly—like a navigator providing real-time feedback on a journey, ensuring the best possible route is taken. Attribution modeling is another AI-driven tool that enhances marketing measurement. By analysing the impact of various channels on conversions, marketers can allocate resources more effectively, maximizing ROI. Understanding which touchpoints contribute most to success allows for strategic decision-making, ensuring that every marketing dollar is well spent.

In today's digital landscape, AI is not just a luxury—it's a necessity for businesses looking to create meaningful customer experiences, drive engagement, and optimize marketing performance. As AI continues to evolve, its role in marketing will only grow, offering even more innovative ways to connect with consumers and enhance business outcomes.

Interactive Element: Reflection Section

Think about a recent online purchase or interaction with a brand that felt exceptionally personalised and seamless. How did AI shape that experience? Whether it was a product recommendation that perfectly matched your needs or a chatbot that resolved your query instantly, AI likely played a role in enhancing your journey. These subtle yet impactful interactions influence how we perceive brands, shaping our trust and engagement with them.

AI is deeply woven into our daily lives, often in ways we don't even notice. From personalised shopping suggestions to tailored music playlists and intuitive search results, AI refines our choices, making experiences more relevant and enjoyable. In marketing, AI goes beyond technology—it's about building genuine connections.

By leveraging personalization, predictive analytics, and advanced measurement tools, businesses engage customers more effectively, transforming marketing from a broad broadcast into a meaningful, one-on-one conversation. AI-driven strategies don't just sell products; they foster loyalty, trust, and long-term relationships by making consumers feel understood.

As AI continues to evolve, its role in marketing will only deepen. Businesses that embrace this technology will gain a competitive edge by anticipating consumer needs, delivering hyper-relevant experiences, and fostering authentic engagement. The future of marketing isn't just data-driven—it's AI-driven, unlocking deeper insights into consumer behavior and creating truly personalised interactions.

Automating Customer Service with AI

Imagine a world where customer service queries are resolved swiftly, without the frustrating back-and-forth that drains time and patience. AI-powered chatbots are making this a reality, transforming customer interactions. These digital assistants efficiently handle routine inquiries, providing instant responses and freeing human agents for more complex tasks. Integrating chatbots with CRM systems enhances personalization by accessing customer data, allowing them to deliver tailored responses that feel anything but automated. This seamless integration ensures that every interaction is relevant and informed, fostering a more satisfying customer experience.

AI isn't just about answering questions—it's about understanding them. Managing customer feedback has evolved from manually sifting through comments to leveraging AI for deep insights. Sentiment analysis tools scan social media and other platforms to capture public opinion, identifying whether feedback is positive, negative, or neutral. This enables businesses to gauge customer satisfaction at a glance. Automatically prioritizing tickets based on urgency ensures pressing issues receive immediate attention, streamlining operations and directing resources where needed.

Self-service portals have become a staple in customer support, and AI is enhancing these platforms dramatically. Imagine a knowledge base that anticipates queries and suggests articles before customers even finish typing. AI-driven recommendations quickly guide users to the correct information, reducing the need for human intervention. Interactive troubleshooting guides take it a step further by walking customers through real-time solutions, empowering them to resolve issues independently. This leads to faster resolutions and increased satisfaction.

Additionally, visual search functionality is rapidly integrating into customer service, allowing users to upload images of products or issues. AI analyses these images to provide precise solutions or product alternatives, significantly enhancing the customer experience, particularly in retail and tech support sectors.

Monitoring service quality is crucial, and AI tools provide continuous assessments of customer interactions. Speech recognition technology analyses call recordings to ensure compliance with service standards, evaluating tone, language, and response times. AI-driven sentiment scoring adds another layer by detecting the emotional nuances of conversations. By understanding how customers feel during interactions, businesses can refine their approach to enhance satisfaction and loyalty.

AI's role in customer service is transformative, blending efficiency and personalization to set new standards for interaction quality. With chatbots handling routine tasks, feedback analysis offering actionable insights, enhanced self-service options empowering customers, and continuous monitoring ensuring high service standards, businesses can deliver exceptional support experiences.

The result is a win-win: Customers enjoy faster resolutions and more personalised interactions, while companies streamline operations and improve efficiency.

AI's integration into customer service isn't about replacing human agents—it's about augmenting their capabilities. By taking over repetitive tasks, AI allows human representatives to focus on complex issues requiring empathy and critical thinking—the areas where humans truly excel. This collaboration between AI and human agents creates a balanced support environment where efficiency meets empathy.

The potential of AI in customer service extends beyond immediate benefits. As these systems learn from each interaction, they become more adept at predicting customer needs and preferences. This predictive capability allows businesses to anticipate issues before they arise, offering proactive solutions that enhance customer loyalty and retention. Imagine a world where your service provider resolves an issue before you even notice it—AI is paving the way for this level of proactive engagement.

As technology continues to evolve, so will AI's capabilities in customer service. From more sophisticated chatbots capable of handling nuanced conversations to advanced feedback analytics that provide deeper insights into customer sentiment, the future holds exciting possibilities. Businesses that embrace these innovations will lead in customer service excellence, setting new benchmarks for speed, personalization, and overall experience quality.

Incorporating AI into customer service strategies requires careful planning and execution. Companies must train AI systems on diverse datasets to avoid biases and inaccuracies. Continuous monitoring and optimization are essential to maintaining high performance and adapting to changing customer needs. Moreover, transparency in AI usage fosters trust, reassuring customers that their data is handled responsibly.

To reinforce ethical AI practices, businesses are adopting AI ethics boards and frameworks, ensuring fairness and accountability. This not only addresses concerns about data privacy but also positions companies as responsible leaders in AI utilization.

AI's impact on customer service is profound, redefining how businesses interact with consumers and setting new standards for efficiency and personalization. With AI-powered chatbots streamlining operations, sentiment analysis providing valuable insights, enhanced self-service portals empowering users, and continuous monitoring ensuring quality assurance, companies can deliver exceptional support experiences that exceed expectations. As these technologies continue to advance, the potential for further enhancements in customer service is limitless.

Enhancing Productivity in Operations Through AI

Imagine stepping into a bustling warehouse where every item has its place, every movement has a purpose, and chaos is a thing of the past. This isn't a fantasy—it's the reality of AI-enhanced supply chain management. By streamlining logistics, AI reduces costs and boosts efficiency. Predictive demand forecasting plays a pivotal role, acting like a crystal ball that anticipates which products will fly off the shelves. This foresight allows businesses to adjust inventory levels, ensuring products are available without overstocking.

Real-time inventory tracking is another game-changer. With IoT integration, companies monitor stock levels and locations with pinpoint accuracy. This approach minimizes waste, maximizes availability, and keeps operations agile.

AI is also revolutionizing quality control. Imagine an assembly line equipped with AI-powered cameras scanning each product for defects. Image recognition technology catches flaws that human eyes might miss, ensuring consistent product quality, reducing returns, and enhancing customer satisfaction. Automated compliance checks further streamline the process by verifying that products meet regulatory standards before they hit the market, saving time and preventing costly errors.

Beyond manufacturing, AI is transforming agriculture. Intelligent irrigation systems analyse weather patterns and soil conditions to determine optimal water usage, conserving resources while improving crop yield and quality.

Resource allocation, often a complex puzzle, is one AI solves with precision. By analysing operational data, AI suggests optimal deployment strategies. Workforce scheduling becomes seamless with predictive analytics, helping businesses allocate staff efficiently and prevent burnout. AI also optimizes energy consumption in manufacturing, identifying patterns and recommending energy-saving measures that lower costs and reduce environmental impact—a win for businesses and the planet.

Process automation is the unsung hero of productivity. AI frees human resources from mundane tasks, allowing them to focus on strategic activities. Robotic process automation (RPA) handles administrative duties with robotic precision, streamlining repetitive tasks like data entry. This not only boosts productivity but also improves job satisfaction by shifting employees to more meaningful work.

AI-driven data entry automation further alleviates workload pressures, reducing errors and accelerating processing times. Imagine spreadsheets populating themselves with minimal oversight—this is AI in action, creating a streamlined operation where efficiency reigns supreme, paving the way for innovation and growth.

AI integration into business operations isn't about replacing human effort—it's about augmenting it. With predictive demand forecasting, real-time tracking, automated quality control, resource optimization, and process automation, businesses transform challenges into opportunities for excellence. These advancements not only enhance productivity but also keep companies competitive in a fast-paced market.

As AI evolves, its potential to revolutionize industries continues to grow. AI-powered climate modeling is already facilitating sustainable practices by predicting environmental changes and optimizing resource consumption.

The impact of AI extends beyond immediate operational benefits—it's shaping the future of work by fostering innovation and adaptability. By embracing these technologies, businesses position themselves at the forefront of industry evolution, ready to tackle new challenges with confidence and creativity.

Visual Element: Infographic

Explore an infographic illustrating AI's role in streamlining supply chain processes. The visual depicts how predictive demand forecasting, real-time inventory tracking, and energy consumption optimization enhance operational efficiency. This visualization helps stakeholders understand how AI technologies can be integrated to form a cohesive and highly efficient operational strategy.

The infographic also highlights successful case studies where companies have leveraged AI to improve logistics and resource management, providing a blueprint for businesses to replicate their success.

As AI continues to evolve, its potential to transform operations grows exponentially. From supply chain management to quality control and resource allocation, AI empowers businesses to operate at peak performance while fostering sustainability and innovation. The result is a dynamic environment where efficiency meets creativity, paving the way for a future where anything is possible.

Financial Forecasting with AI Tools

Imagine a world where you could predict financial market trends with remarkable accuracy. Thanks to AI, this isn't just a fantasy. AI models now play a pivotal role in forecasting economic trends, offering insights that inform strategic decision-making. Machine learning algorithms analyse historical data and market conditions to identify patterns and predict stock price movements, much like a seasoned trader anticipating shifts. Armed with this data, investors can make informed decisions, minimizing risks and maximizing returns.

AI-driven economic forecasting adds another layer of precision to financial planning. By sifting through vast datasets, AI predicts economic trends, helping businesses prepare for changes in demand or supply chain disruptions. It's like having a financial soothsayer, guiding organizations through uncertainty with data-backed confidence. These forecasts enable proactive strategy adjustments, ensuring resilience in volatile economic conditions.

Risk management is another domain where AI proves invaluable. Identifying and mitigating financial risks is essential for businesses navigating today's complex landscape. AI enhances credit risk assessment by evaluating vast amounts of data to determine creditworthiness, helping lenders make smarter decisions and reducing default rates. In banking, AI-powered fraud detection acts as a vigilant sentinel, constantly scanning transactions for anomalies and flagging potential fraud in real time. This safeguards financial institutions and customers alike.

AI also streamlines financial reporting, traditionally a labor-intensive and error-prone process. Automated tools ensure accuracy and efficiency, providing real-time financial insights that help businesses stay on top of their financial health. Compliance reporting benefits from AI's precision, reducing the burden on finance teams while ensuring regulatory adherence.

Sustainable investing and ESG (Environmental, Social, Governance) considerations are becoming integral to financial strategies. AI analyses vast ESG data points, enabling investors to assess companies' sustainability practices and align their portfolios with ethical standards. This fusion of financial returns and societal impact is shaping the future of responsible investing.

Investment strategy execution is also undergoing a transformation with AI. Portfolio optimization algorithms analyse market data to recommend asset allocations that balance risk and reward. Think of it as having a personal investment advisor with an encyclopedic knowledge of market dynamics. Meanwhile, AI-driven trading bots provide real-time market analysis and execute trades based on predefined criteria, allowing investors to capitalize on opportunities with precision.

AI's integration into financial forecasting isn't just about number-crunching—it's reshaping how we understand and interact with financial markets. By providing deeper insights into trends and risks, AI empowers businesses and investors to make smarter, more agile decisions. The ability to anticipate changes and adapt strategies ensures organizations stay competitive in an ever-evolving financial landscape.

For those looking to sharpen their financial acumen, embracing AI tools offers a distinct advantage. Understanding these technologies and applying them effectively allows individuals and businesses to navigate the complexities of finance with greater confidence. Whether managing personal investments or steering a corporate portfolio, AI delivers the insights needed to stay ahead.

Looking ahead, AI's potential in financial forecasting will expand with advancements in quantum computing, enabling the rapid analysis of even larger datasets and uncovering correlations invisible to classical systems. This evolution promises even greater accuracy and sophistication in financial predictions.

AI in finance isn't about replacing human intuition—it's about augmenting it with data-driven insights that enhance decision-making at every level. From predicting market trends to optimizing investments and managing risks, AI is a powerful tool for those looking to thrive in today's fast-paced financial environment. The key to success lies in understanding these tools and leveraging them effectively to achieve your financial goals.

Building an AI-Driven Business Strategy

Creating an AI roadmap is like setting the GPS for your business journey. The first step is identifying key areas where AI can make a real impact—whether it's streamlining operations, enhancing customer service, or driving innovation. Once these areas are pinpointed, set clear, measurable goals. Do you want AI to increase sales, improve customer satisfaction, or optimize efficiency? Defining these objectives gives your AI initiatives direction and purpose, ensuring they're not just tech experiments but strategic tools that drive success.

Aligning AI projects with business goals is essential. If revenue growth is the priority, AI can enhance sales through smarter targeting or optimized inventory management. If customer experience is the focus, AI-powered personalization or faster service solutions can be game-changers. This strategic alignment ensures AI initiatives contribute meaningfully to the bottom line rather than becoming disconnected tech investments.

AI also fosters innovation by encouraging businesses to experiment and adapt. Establishing AI competency centers or innovation hubs within the organization creates a space for exploring AI applications and generating ideas that integrate seamlessly into existing processes. A culture of innovation accelerates AI adoption and unlocks new possibilities.

Cross-departmental collaboration is crucial for maximizing AI's potential. When teams from different areas work together on AI projects, they bring diverse insights that lead to creative, practical solutions. Breaking down silos and fostering open communication allows ideas to flow freely. Equally important is equipping employees with AI training and resources, empowering them to use AI tools confidently and effectively.

Measuring AI project success goes beyond performance metrics. While data-driven insights are valuable, the real question is whether AI initiatives achieve their intended impact. Did they enhance efficiency? Improve customer engagement? Drive profitability? Continuous feedback loops help refine AI strategies, ensuring ongoing improvement and alignment with business needs. Think of it as fine-tuning an instrument until it harmonizes perfectly with your company's objectives.

Incorporating these strategies into your business plan lays the foundation for successful AI integration. A well-structured roadmap, goal alignment, innovation culture, and continuous evaluation create an environment where AI thrives, enhancing efficiency and driving growth.

An iterative approach is key—regularly testing AI strategies and adjusting based on performance and shifting market conditions ensures long-term viability. AI is not just about adopting new technology; it's about transforming business operations and maintaining a competitive edge in today's fast-paced world.

As we move forward, we'll explore how AI is reshaping the future of work, redefining roles, and creating new career opportunities. Get ready to navigate this exciting frontier as we uncover how AI is revolutionizing workplaces and the skills needed to succeed in this evolving landscape.

Chapter 4

Everyday Life with AI

Smart Homes: AI-Powered Conveniences

Imagine stepping into a world where your home intuitively recognizes your presence and adapts to your needs. Picture this: as you walk through the door, the lights automatically illuminate, the thermostat adjusts to your ideal temperature, and your favorite music plays softly in the background. This isn't a scene from a sci-fi movie—it's the reality of smart home technology today. With artificial intelligence at its core, modern homes are transforming daily routines into seamless, personalised experiences.

At the heart of this revolution are voice-activated assistants like Amazon Alexa and Google Home. These AI-powered hubs allow you to control everything—from lighting to security systems—using simple voice commands. Need to check the weather, set reminders, or play your favorite playlist? Just ask. These assistants continuously learn from your habits, fine-tuning their responses and automating tasks to match your preferences, making them indispensable companions in modern living.

Expanding on this integration, AI-powered homes now feature an extensive range of smart devices. From refrigerators that track food expiration dates to intelligent blinds that adjust based on natural light, every element of your home works in harmony. This interconnected ecosystem isn't just about convenience—it's about creating a living space that seamlessly adapts to your lifestyle.

Beyond voice commands, AI enables intelligent lighting systems that adjust based on occupancy and time of day. These systems dim or brighten automatically, setting the perfect ambiance for relaxation or productivity. Motion sensors detect unoccupied rooms and turn off lights, reducing electricity waste and cutting energy costs. Some systems even leverage predictive algorithms that factor in weather patterns—preemptively heating your home before a cold front arrives or cooling it ahead of a heatwave. This not only ensures comfort but also enhances energy efficiency.

Security takes a giant leap forward with AI-driven surveillance and access control. Imagine a system that recognizes familiar faces and alerts you only when it detects an unknown visitor. Facial recognition technology differentiates between family members and potential intruders, enhancing safety without unnecessary notifications. Smart locks with biometric access add another layer of security, allowing you to grant temporary access to guests or service providers without handing over physical keys.

For frequent travelers, AI-powered location-based security features provide real-time alerts if someone accesses your home while you're away. These digital safeguards offer peace of mind, ensuring that you're immediately informed of any unusual activity and can take action from anywhere in the world.

Beyond convenience and security, AI plays a crucial role in sustainability. Smart thermostats like Nest learn your schedule and preferences, optimizing heating and cooling to reduce energy consumption without compromising comfort. These devices even generate automated energy reports, highlighting areas where you can cut costs. When integrated with smart grid technology, AI-powered homes can communicate with utility providers to determine the best times for energy use, reducing strain on the grid during peak hours and lowering electricity bills.

Household chores are also becoming effortless thanks to AI-driven automation. Robot vacuum cleaners equipped with intelligent mapping technology navigate around obstacles, clean efficiently, and return to their charging docks automatically. In the kitchen, AI-powered grocery management systems track inventory and suggest recipes based on available ingredients, minimizing food waste and simplifying meal prep.

Even laundry is getting smarter. AI-enabled washing machines now analyse fabric type and load weight to optimize water and detergent use, extending the lifespan of clothes while conserving resources. Some machines can even detect fabric wear and recommend gentle cycles to prevent premature damage—a small but impactful step toward sustainable living.

With AI at the helm, smart homes are no longer just about automation; they represent a shift toward more efficient, secure, and eco-friendly living. As technology continues to evolve, our homes will become even more intuitive, adapting seamlessly to our routines, preferences, and environmental needs. The future of living isn't just smart—it's intelligent.

Interactive Element: Reflection Section

Imagine stepping into a home where technology effortlessly enhances your daily routine. Your coffee brews at the perfect strength just as you wake up, the shower is preheated to your preferred temperature, and as you get ready, an AI assistant updates you on your schedule, traffic conditions, and the latest news. This isn't a distant future—it's the reality that AI-powered smart homes are bringing to life today.

Think about the tasks you'd love to automate. Would you enjoy a thermostat that adjusts itself based on the weather? Lights that dim automatically as bedtime approaches? Or a security system that recognizes familiar faces and alerts you only when something unusual happens? AI technology is redefining home living, offering seamless convenience, enhanced security, and optimized energy use.

Beyond simplifying routines, AI-powered homes can adapt to your lifestyle, learning your preferences and anticipating your needs. From managing energy consumption efficiently to automating household chores, these intelligent environments do more than just respond—they proactively enhance your quality of life.

As AI continues to evolve, the possibilities expand exponentially. By embracing these innovations, we move toward a future where technology integrates effortlessly with our personal spaces, creating homes that are not only smart but truly intuitive.

Health and Wellness: AI as a Personal Assistant

Consider the tiny wearable device on your wrist, tracking every step you take and each calorie you burn. Gadgets like Fitbit have revolutionized personal health monitoring, enabling users to gather a wealth of data about their fitness levels. These wearables use AI to analyse activity patterns, offering insights that help optimize workouts and achieve fitness goals. By learning from your habits, they provide personalised feedback and suggest ways to improve your health routine. Imagine receiving a nudge to take a brisk walk after a sedentary day or being congratulated on reaching a new milestone. These devices transform raw data into meaningful insights, encouraging healthier lifestyles.

Moreover, wearable technology isn't just limited to tracking steps or calories. Advancements in the field have led to devices capable of monitoring heart rate variability, sleep quality, and even blood oxygen levels, offering a comprehensive picture of overall health. With such detailed insights, these devices not only monitor but also actively guide users toward better health decisions, serving as trusted companions in their fitness journeys.

Recent innovations in wearable technology have introduced capabilities like ECG monitoring, which can detect irregular heart rhythms and early signs of atrial fibrillation, providing vital information that could help prevent cardiac events. With features like fall detection, these wearables offer peace of mind, especially for elderly users at risk of falls. Looking ahead, advancements may allow wearables to detect early symptoms of illnesses like the flu by analysing temperature fluctuations and activity level shifts—marking a step toward preemptive health management.

Virtual health assistants are another way AI integrates into daily life, acting as helpful companions for managing health-related tasks. Think of AI chatbots that schedule medical appointments with just a few taps on your phone, streamlining the process and eliminating the need to wait on hold. Additionally, medication reminders ensure you never miss a dose. Tracking apps use AI to monitor adherence to prescribed treatments, sending gentle prompts to keep users on track. This is especially beneficial for those managing chronic conditions, offering peace of mind and improved health outcomes through regular oversight.

Chronic condition management has taken another leap forward with integrated platforms that sync data across various devices, creating a centralized health profile that can be shared with healthcare providers. This continuity enhances patient care and ensures comprehensive oversight of one's health progress. Imagine walking into a medical consultation where your recent health stats are automatically uploaded to the doctor's system, minimizing guesswork and allowing for more precise diagnostics.

AI's role in mental health is equally transformative. Cognitive behavioral therapy (CBT) apps provide accessible, on-the-go support for mental well-being. These AI-driven platforms offer exercises and techniques used in traditional therapy, helping users manage stress, anxiety, and depression. By engaging with these apps, individuals can work through challenges at their own pace, making mental health care more accessible. Mood-tracking applications further enhance this support by analysing emotional patterns over time. They offer AI-driven insights into potential mood triggers, empowering users to better understand and manage their mental health.

Moreover, using natural language processing, some advanced apps can interpret user entries to detect signs of mental distress, offer proactive coping strategies, or suggest when it might be time to seek external support. This level of assistance serves as a lifeline for many, fostering a deeper understanding of one's psychological state and promoting better self-regulation. Envision a future where AI plays a proactive role, detecting subtle shifts in mood that signal when timely interventions could prevent deeper mental health struggles.

Nutrition also benefits from AI's capabilities. Personalised nutrition planning is now a reality, with apps analysing dietary habits and suggesting meal plans tailored to individual health goals. Whether you aim to lose weight, build muscle, or maintain a balanced diet, these apps consider your preferences and restrictions, offering meal suggestions that align with your objectives. Imagine an app that learns your tastes over time and suggests recipes that not only meet your nutritional needs but also delight your taste buds.

Furthermore, AI applications now employ visual recognition to log dietary intake using smartphone cameras, analysing pictures of meals to provide an accurate nutritional breakdown. This eliminates the guesswork often associated with maintaining food diaries, providing more precise data for better nutritional planning. In the near future, anticipate features that recommend portion adjustments based on metabolic needs and activity levels, ensuring continuous nutritional alignment.

Interactive Element: Reflection Section

Think about how AI could support your health and wellness journey. Are there specific areas where you need assistance, such as staying active or managing stress? Consider how AI tools might provide solutions tailored to your lifestyle and goals.

These innovations in health and wellness are more than just technological advancements; they mark a shift toward proactive, personalised care. By integrating seamlessly into daily routines, AI empowers individuals to take charge of their health in meaningful ways. Whether through wearables that keep you moving, virtual assistants that simplify healthcare management, or mental health apps that offer support when you need it most, AI is becoming an essential part of self-care.

The future of health and wellness looks promising as these technologies continue to evolve, catering to individual needs and making well-being more accessible for everyone. As AI advances, imagine the added dimension of predictive health forecasts—offering insights into potential lifestyle adjustments needed to maintain optimal health.

AI in Education: Personalised Learning Paths

Imagine stepping into a classroom where every student learns at their own pace, exploring subjects that spark their curiosity while receiving the support they need. AI is making this vision a reality by personalizing educational experiences to fit individual learning styles. Adaptive learning platforms like DreamBox are leading this transformation, using AI to analyse student interactions and adjust lessons in real time. Whether a student struggles with fractions or excels in algebra, the platform adapts, ensuring engagement remains high while minimizing frustration.

Beyond content customization, AI is revolutionizing study plans through performance analytics. By tracking progress across tasks and assessments, these systems craft personalised study schedules, focusing on strengthening weaknesses and building on strengths. It's like having a dedicated tutor who knows precisely where to direct your efforts for maximum improvement. This tailored approach empowers students, boosting confidence and fostering a lifelong love of learning.

AI enhances not just individual learning but also classroom dynamics. AI-supported collaboration tools, such as automated group work platforms, ensure balanced participation by analysing contributions and promoting equitable teamwork. This fosters fairness and inclusion, amplifying diverse voices in group projects and cultivating an environment where every student feels heard and valued.

Teachers also benefit from AI's capabilities. Automated grading systems handle routine assessments, allowing educators to focus on deeper, more meaningful instruction. AI chatbots act as virtual assistants, promptly addressing student inquiries, clarifying homework assignments, and guiding research projects. These innovations free up teachers' time, enhancing overall classroom efficiency.

Additionally, AI-powered professional development tools analyse teaching patterns and provide educators with personalised resources to refine their methods. With AI monitoring classroom engagement and suggesting activity shifts when energy levels dip, teaching becomes more dynamic and responsive.

Beyond traditional classrooms, AI supports lifelong learning and professional growth. Platforms like Coursera leverage AI to curate online courses tailored to individual career aspirations, helping learners upskill or transition into new fields. Skill assessment tools further refine this process, evaluating existing competencies and recommending areas for development. With AI as a guide, learners can navigate career advancement with confidence, benefiting from real-time insights aligned with industry trends.

AI also fosters inclusivity by breaking barriers to education. Real-time translation tools empower non-native speakers, ensuring language is never an obstacle to learning. Assistive technologies support students with disabilities, from speech recognition software for the hearing impaired to text-to-speech applications for visually impaired learners. These innovations make education more accessible to all.

In resource-limited areas, AI serves as an equalizer, providing remote access to expert educators and quality learning tools. AI-driven virtual classrooms bridge geographical divides, ensuring students in underserved regions receive the same opportunities as their urban counterparts. Imagine the transformative power of AI in remote communities, unlocking potential where traditional education infrastructure falls short.

The integration of AI in education isn't just about technology—it's about reimagining how we learn and teach. By personalizing learning paths, supporting educators, promoting lifelong education, and fostering inclusivity, AI is reshaping the future of education. As we embrace its potential, we move toward an era where quality education is a universal right, powered by innovation and accessibility.

Visual Element: Infographic

Explore an infographic illustrating the transformative role of AI in education. The visual highlights how adaptive learning platforms personalise content, AI tools support teachers, and inclusive technologies remove barriers for diverse learners.

In this evolving educational paradigm, AI serves as both an enabler and a guide. Its ability to adapt to individual needs makes learning more engaging and effective, while its support for educators enhances teaching practices. As we continue to embrace these advancements, the future of education looks brighter than ever—one where every learner has the opportunity to succeed on their own terms.

The possibilities AI brings to education are boundless. Each tool and technology has the potential to revolutionise the way knowledge is shared and acquired. By welcoming these changes, we open doors to new ways of thinking and understanding—a true testament to the power of innovation in shaping our world for the better.

Travel Planning Simplified with AI Tools

Imagine planning your next holiday with an assistant who knows you almost better than you know yourself. AI has revolutionised travel by providing personalised recommendations tailored to your preferences. Whether you're a beach lover or a mountain seeker, AI travel apps analyse your past trips, browsing history, and even social media activity to suggest destinations that match your style. Platforms like TripIt organise your itineraries, pulling details from confirmation emails and creating a seamless travel plan. No more juggling multiple apps or stressing over missed details. And when it comes to flights and accommodation, AI's dynamic pricing alerts ensure you secure the best deals by notifying you of price drops. It's like having a savvy travel agent in your pocket, helping you save money while maximising your travel experience.

Safety is a top priority when travelling, and AI plays a crucial role in ensuring secure journeys. AI-assisted navigation systems provide real-time traffic updates and alternative routes, helping you avoid delays and congestion. These systems not only save time but also enhance safety by guiding you through less-travelled paths when necessary. Predictive analytics further bolster travel safety by assessing risks associated with specific destinations. They consider factors such as weather forecasts, political stability, and health advisories, offering insights that enable you to make informed decisions. It's like having a knowledgeable guide who monitors potential hazards, ensuring your travel experience remains smooth and worry-free.

Booking travel can often feel like a daunting task, with countless options and variables to consider. However, AI streamlines this process by automating reservations for flights and hotels through chatbots. These virtual assistants handle inquiries and bookings swiftly, ensuring seamless transactions without human intervention. Imagine having a conversation with a chatbot that finds you the best flight options based on your schedule and budget, then completes the booking within minutes. Additionally, AI-driven expense management tools track your travel expenses effortlessly, categorising them for easy reporting. This automation reduces administrative burdens and ensures you stay within budget while enjoying your trip.

As AI takes over logistical nuances, travellers can focus more on personalising their journeys. Platforms now provide experiential suggestions based on your past itinerary, offering culinary tours, guided expeditions, and local events that align with your interests. Imagine the thrill of embarking on a trip where each day unfolds with activities and sights that reflect your personal travel ethos.

Travelling to foreign lands often comes with language barriers that can hinder exploration and interaction. AI becomes a trusty companion by offering real-time language translation apps that instantly break down communication barriers. Picture yourself in a bustling market abroad—simply speak into your phone, and the app seamlessly translates your words into the local language. This instant translation fosters meaningful connections with locals and enriches your cultural experiences. Beyond language assistance, AI provides cultural etiquette tips tailored to each destination. These insights help you navigate social norms respectfully, ensuring positive interactions with locals and avoiding unintentional faux pas.

AI also supports the growing trend of sustainable travel. Apps provide insights into eco-friendly accommodation and activities, aligning your travel itinerary with environmental consciousness. Imagine an app that optimises your choice of transport, showing the most time-efficient rail routes to minimise your carbon footprint.

Visual Element: Infographic

Explore an infographic detailing how AI is transforming travel planning. The visual highlights personalised recommendations, safety features, booking automation, and cultural assistance, illustrating how AI enhances every aspect of your travel journey.

Incorporating AI into travel planning isn't just about convenience—it's about enriching every facet of the experience. From personalised recommendations that align with your interests to safety features that keep you secure on the road, AI brings unprecedented ease and enjoyment to exploring new destinations. Streamlined booking processes eliminate stress, allowing you to focus on the excitement of the journey ahead. Meanwhile, language and cultural assistance ensure you connect deeply with the places and people you encounter along the way. With AI as your travel companion, every trip becomes an adventure worth savouring, where the seamless blending of expectation and discovery turns travel into an art form.

AI in Entertainment: Tailoring Your Experience

Imagine settling in for the evening, remote in hand, and your streaming service greets you with a selection of shows and movies that seem curated just for you. This isn't a coincidence; it's AI's magic at work. Streaming giants like Netflix utilise sophisticated algorithms to analyse your viewing habits. They consider what you've watched and rated and even how long you've lingered on a title before pressing play. This data helps them tailor recommendations, ensuring the next suggestion is something you're likely to enjoy. It's like having a personal assistant who knows your taste in entertainment better than anyone else.

When it comes to music, AI-driven recommendation engines are equally transformative. Services like Spotify and Apple Music learn from your listening habits, curating playlists that suit your mood and preferences. They consider factors like the genre of songs you frequently replay and those you skip after a few seconds. This creates a dynamic listening experience that evolves with you, introducing new artists and tracks that align with your changing musical interests. With each play and skip, the system becomes more attuned to your unique preferences.

Moving beyond traditional forms of media, AI has begun to make waves in the ever-expanding realm of virtual influencers. These AI-generated personas engage audiences across social platforms, offering fresh perspectives and unique content, blurring the lines between human influencers and digital marvels. Imagine an influencer whose insights are guided by trends captured in real time, responding directly and immediately to shifts in global interests.

Interactive gaming experiences have also leapt forward thanks to AI. Imagine playing a video game where the non-player characters (NPCs) adapt their behaviour based on your actions. AI drives these characters to make decisions that enrich gameplay, offering fresh and engaging challenges every time you play. In open-world games, procedural content generation enabled by AI ensures that no two playthroughs are ever the same. This technology generates vast landscapes and intricate storylines on the fly, responding to player choices and creating a personalised adventure tailored to your style, enhancing your engagement with seemingly alive and aware environments.

AI's influence extends beyond gaming into the creative realms of art and media. Consider music composition tools that assist budding musicians in crafting melodies and harmonies. These AI-powered platforms suggest chord progressions and arrangement ideas, sparking creativity and helping artists overcome writer's block. Similarly, automated video editing software leverages AI to offer editing suggestions based on footage content, enhancing storytelling by identifying key moments and recommending transitions or effects that enhance the narrative.

Experimentations with AI-created art have opened new frontiers in creativity, allowing enthusiasts to generate novel visual masterpieces or experiment with AI-driven photography enhancement tools that bring images to vivid life. Imagine a future where artists and AI collaborate seamlessly, giving birth to new art forms that redefine expression.

Virtual reality (VR) is another frontier where AI has made significant strides. Imagine donning a VR headset and stepping into a world where every detail feels crafted just for you. AI enhances VR experiences by analysing user interactions in real time and adjusting environments to optimise immersion. Whether it's tweaking the lighting for a more atmospheric scene or modifying NPC behaviour to suit your playstyle, AI's real-time adjustments ensure that each VR session is unique and deeply engaging, marking a turning point in experiential narratives where every action is met with an immersive reality shift perfectly aligned with personal hopes.

As the lines between virtual and physical worlds continue to blur, AI serves as the mechanic behind the scenes, adjusting experiences to resonate personally with each participant. This makes digital escapades a reflection of individual tastes and preferences. I look forward to integrative VR experiences in which AI recreates real-world scenarios with stunning authenticity, allowing users to explore cultural landmarks before actually visiting them.

The integration of AI in entertainment isn't just about convenience or novelty; it's about creating experiences that resonate on a personal level. By understanding individual preferences, AI makes entertainment more accessible and enjoyable. Whether you're discovering new music, exploring virtual worlds, or enjoying personalised content recommendations, AI tailors each interaction to fit you perfectly.

As we wrap up this chapter on AI in everyday life, it's clear that these technologies are not just transforming how we live but also how we relax and enjoy our leisure time. From customised playlists to immersive gaming adventures, AI enriches the tapestry of our daily experiences. In the next chapter, we'll explore how AI is shaping industries and professions, redefining what it means to work in a world where technology continually evolves alongside us. Stay tuned for insights into how AI's influence extends beyond personal spaces into the broader professional landscape. Embark on this next journey to understand how AI prepares industries for a future as dynamic and individually engaging as our own personal experiences with the evolution of technology.

Chapter 5

Visualizing AI Concepts

Visualizing Data: The Role of AI in Business Intelligence

Imagine standing amidst the awe-inspiring atmosphere of a concert, enveloped by the enchanting orchestration of lights and music. This mesmerising fusion transcends mere entertainment; it's an expertly crafted masterpiece designed to create unforgettable impressions. Likewise, data visualisation through the lens of AI turns complex datasets into artistic representations, transforming what might be indecipherable arrays in a spreadsheet into engaging narratives. The task of decoding these intricate clusters of numbers becomes a storytelling journey wherein AI's intelligent algorithms birth vivid narratives, providing clarity and understanding that is both engaging and enriching.

AI's transformative prowess in this domain hinges on enhancing how data is perceived and interpreted. In today's business landscape, AI-enabled dashboards are vital components of business intelligence tools, elevating data presentations to an art form. They present information not only in visually appealing ways but also with a precision that illuminates trends and patterns, ensuring they are not overlooked. These dashboards function as centralised hubs, empowering users to monitor real-time performance metrics. This real-time capability allows decision-makers to identify opportunities and potential inaccuracies, ensuring strategic flexibility swiftly. These dashboards are far from static; they invite active engagement, allowing users to click into specific data points for deeper insights or tap into hidden patterns. This interactive experience fosters a deeper understanding of data, enhancing decision-making and strategic planning.

When visualised beyond aesthetic dimensions, AI provides invaluable insights that might otherwise be easily missed. By harnessing predictive analytics, AI visualisations offer a window into the future by utilising historical data to predict future trends and outcomes. Imagine a sales manager equipped with such insights: predicting high-demand products during festive seasons becomes pivotal, enabling effective stock management and marketing strategies. Furthermore, AI facilitates real-time data tracking and instant alerts, allowing businesses to respond proactively to market fluctuations, thus maintaining a competitive edge in the constantly evolving business landscape.

Several powerful tools harness the power of AI to streamline data visualisation efforts. For instance, Tableau enriches data exploration with AI-driven insights, making data interaction more intuitive and user-empowering. Features like natural language processing enable users to pose questions in ordinary language and receive visual responses, breaking down the barriers to data comprehension. Similarly, Power BI integrates advanced analytics and machine learning capabilities, enabling users to extract deeper insights without requiring extensive technical knowledge. Thus, Power BI democratises access to valuable information.

The impact of visualised data on business strategy is profound and far-reaching. When data is depicted vividly and engagingly, aligning stakeholders on strategic goals becomes a seamless process, facilitating effective communication. Visual reports become indispensable assets in presentations, effectively conveying complex information succinctly and persuasively. They bridge the communicative gap between data scientists and business leaders, ensuring a unified understanding when crucial decisions must be made. From a market analysis standpoint, data-driven strategies become clearer as visualised trends illuminate promising opportunities or spotlight potential risks, facilitating proactive measures and methods.

Visual Element: Interactive Exercise

To delve deeper into these concepts, embark on the journey of creating your own AI-driven dashboard using freely accessible online tools. Experiment with diverse datasets to witness firsthand how visualisation metamorphoses raw data into engaging stories, enabling enhanced decision-making capabilities and strategic foresight.

By fully embracing AI-enhanced data visualisation, businesses unlock new dimensions of understanding and foresight. These tools transcend technical barriers, offering user-friendly experiences accessible to all. Whether the goal is analysing sales metrics or evaluating customer interactions, AI-powered visualisations provide the clarity required to drive success. Data visualisation goes beyond simple aesthetics; it transforms data into actionable insights, turning numbers into narratives that not only inform but inspire.

As we further explore AI's role in visualisation, consider its immense potential in clarifying complexities and enhancing decision-making across countless sectors and facets of life.

Infographics: Simplifying AI Trends and Predictions

Imagine deciphering a dense, jargon-filled article on AI trends—it's daunting, and you yearn for clarity amidst the complexity. Enter infographics, a beacon of clarity in the often-confusing labyrinth of AI information. Infographics distil AI's intricate sphere into vivid, eye-catching visuals that convey information efficiently. Consider the challenge of comparing AI adoption across various industries. Instead of laboriously parsing through pages of text, an infographic succinctly presents this data, quickly revealing which sectors are leading AI integration and where burgeoning opportunities lie.

Visual timelines that trace AI's technological evolution add additional layers of depth. They present a panoramic view of AI's journey from inception to present-day innovations, highlighting critical milestones—akin to viewing a movie trailer and grasping the storyline's essence. The power of well-crafted visuals lies in their capacity to capture the essence of extensive narratives with brevity and clarity.

Infographics excel in demystifying AI's core complexities, making them accessible to broad audiences. Consider the intricate mechanism of machine learning, often perceived as a tangled web of algorithms and data. A well-crafted flowchart can demystify this process, demonstrating how data inputs transform into predictive outputs. These visualisations bridge the gap between theoretical concepts and real-world applications, fostering deeper comprehension and engagement.

Moreover, infographics effectively juxtapose AI capabilities against human faculties. Visual comparisons between AI systems' data processing and human cognitive approaches shed light on AI's strengths and limitations, cultivating a thorough understanding of AI's role across multiple domains.

In the future, infographics could project AI trends across specific sectors such as healthcare or finance, predicting transformative impacts like refined diagnostics or personalised medicine. Such forecasts equip us with foresight, preparing us for forthcoming challenges and opportunities.

Infographics mapping AI-driven career trajectories provide yet another compelling application. These visuals elucidate shifts in job roles due to automation, pinpointing positions likely to gain prominence or face obsolescence. This foresight proves invaluable for individuals seeking to future-proof their skills and career paths.

The power of infographics lies in their ability to condense, clarify, and embed information in lasting visuals. A single image can articulate what might otherwise require thousands of words, especially when grappling with complex data. Infographics are ideal for encapsulating AI statistics, serving as concise reference guides that linger in memory longer than text alone. They break down vast data archives into digestible visuals, enhancing recall and the practical application of acquired insights.

For organisations venturing into AI, visual guides that depict AI implementation strategies provide significant insights. Imagine a roadmap laying out step-by-step AI integration with visual touchpoints and best practices. These guides simplify elaborate processes and offer tangible steps towards successful deployment.

Reflection Section: Create Your Own Infographic

Reflect on a recent AI trend or concept that interests you. Sketch an infographic to articulate this topic, prioritising key points and their compelling visual representation.

While infographics are visually appealing, their true strength lies in simplifying complexities and making information more accessible to a wider audience. As you explore current trends or anticipate future shifts, these visuals provide clarity in often bewildering contexts. On your immersive journey through the AI domain, stay attuned to infographics that can deepen your understanding and enrich your insights into this transformative field.

Make a Difference with Your Review

"The smallest act of kindness is worth more than the grandest intention." - Oscar Wilde

Helping others brings happiness, and your review can make that happen!

Could you take a moment to help someone just like you—curious about artificial intelligence but not sure how to start?

My goal with *Master AI for Beginners* is to make learning about artificial intelligence easy, fun, and useful for everyone.

But to reach more people, I need your support.

Most readers decide to buy a book based on reviews. Your honest review could help someone else:

...discover new career opportunities. ...feel confident at work or school. ...simplify their daily tasks with AI. ...turn their curiosity into knowledge. ...change their life through the power of AI.

Leaving a review is free, takes just a minute, and can truly make a difference. Simply scan the QR code or visit the link below to share your thoughts:

https://www.amazon.com/dp/B0F59SQ3R8

Thank you for helping others explore and enjoy AI. You're amazing!
Charlie Hansen

Chapter 6

Ethical AI and Its Implications

Privacy Concerns in AI: What You Need to Know

Imagine scrolling through your favourite social media platform and suddenly encountering an advertisement for a product you just discussed with a friend. It feels eerily as though the app is eavesdropping on your conversations. This scenario perfectly illustrates the pervasive presence of AI and its reliance on vast datasets, which are raising significant privacy concerns. Data has become a vital currency in the digital era, but it also carries substantial implications. The collection and storage of sensitive information expose individuals to numerous threats, such as data breaches and unauthorised access. Personal details, from browsing habits to health records, are amassed in expansive databases that remain vulnerable to cyber intrusions. Understanding these potential ramifications is crucial as AI-driven technologies become increasingly integrated into our everyday lives.

Regulatory frameworks such as Europe's General Data Protection Regulation (GDPR) and the California Consumer Privacy Act (CCPA) have been established to safeguard privacy. These regulations define how companies can collect, store, and utilise personal data. For instance, the GDPR imposes stringent rules on data processing and grants individuals greater control over their personal information. Similarly, the CCPA mandates transparency, enabling individuals to understand the data collected about them. While these frameworks hold companies accountable, they also present particular challenges for AI development. Balancing privacy and innovation requires careful navigation of these regulations, as legal adaptations often struggle to keep pace with rapid technological advancements.

To preserve privacy in AI applications, implementing best practices is essential. Data anonymisation techniques remove personal identifiers from datasets, allowing AI systems to analyse information without compromising individual privacy. This approach enables companies to extract insights while protecting sensitive data. Additionally, encryption protocols strengthen security, ensuring that data transmission remains private and safeguarded against unauthorised access. When data is encrypted, even if intercepted, it remains unintelligible without the correct decryption key. Adopting such strategies is fundamental to protecting personal information while harnessing AI's potential.

However, privacy protection is not solely a technical issue—it requires a multifaceted approach that intertwines technology with robust policies, corporate responsibility, and individual vigilance. Companies must foster a culture of privacy-first thinking, embedding it within their organisational ethos. Training programmes focused on data privacy and ethics can empower employees to uphold these values, ensuring comprehensive protection that extends beyond technological measures. On an individual level, cultivating digital literacy is paramount. Users must be educated about their online footprint, understanding how their data is collected and used across various platforms. Advocacy initiatives can drive this educational push, raising awareness about privacy rights and encouraging more cautious engagement with digital ecosystems.

Yet, maintaining the delicate balance between privacy and innovation often involves ethical trade-offs. Privacy restrictions can limit AI's potential by restricting access to the vast datasets needed to train sophisticated models. Personalised services, such as tailored recommendations, rely heavily on user data to improve accuracy. Without detailed information, AI systems may struggle to deliver the same level of customisation. Conversely, ethical dilemmas arise when innovation is prioritised over privacy. While personalised experiences enhance convenience, they simultaneously increase the risk of unwarranted intrusions into private spaces.

Reflection Exercise: Balancing Privacy and Innovation

Reflect on a recent interaction you had with an AI-driven service that impressed you with its level of personalisation. What data might have been used to craft that experience, and how do you feel about sharing such information? Consider the balance between personalisation and privacy—how does it impact your overall trust and comfort with the service?

Navigating these ethical dilemmas requires ongoing dialogue and collaboration among stakeholders. As consumers, we must advocate for transparency regarding how our data is utilised. Companies should prioritise developing AI systems that respect privacy while delivering innovative solutions. This endeavour involves designing algorithms that maximise utility without sacrificing user trust. By fostering a culture centred around ethical AI development, we can create technologies that empower individuals without compromising their fundamental rights.

Privacy concerns in AI extend beyond technical challenges; they emerge as societal issues demanding our attention. As AI becomes more embedded in daily routines, understanding these implications enables individuals to make informed decisions about their interactions with technology. Finding a middle ground where innovation flourishes without undermining personal freedoms is essential.

In this ever-evolving landscape, education plays a pivotal role. Staying informed about privacy rights and best practices equips individuals to actively shape AI's future. Engaging in discussions about ethical AI use ensures that diverse voices contribute to the development process. Together, we can forge a balance that respects both privacy and progress in this rapidly advancing field.

Algorithmic Bias: Identifying and Mitigating Risks

Algorithmic bias in AI can be likened to a concealed flaw in an otherwise seamless fabric. It manifests when AI systems produce outcomes that unconsciously favour certain groups, leading to unjust results. This bias often originates from skewed training data, wherein historical prejudices subtly infiltrate algorithms. Consider an AI tool trained on historical hiring decisions from a time when diversity was not prioritised. The system might inadvertently perpetuate those biases, favouring candidates who resemble those previously chosen, thereby excluding equally qualified individuals from diverse backgrounds.

Sources of bias in AI systems vary, but they frequently trace back to the data itself. Historical data reflecting societal biases can taint algorithms. For instance, if a dataset predominantly features one demographic, an AI model might struggle to accurately represent others. This lack of representation skews results, significantly impacting fairness. Incomplete datasets introduce bias by failing to capture the full spectrum of scenarios an AI system might encounter akin to a recipe missing key ingredients, leading to an imbalanced final outcome.

Addressing these issues requires detecting and assessing bias in AI models. Statistical methods highlight discrepancies and imbalances within datasets, serving as an entry point for identifying potential biases. Bias auditing tools and frameworks offer structured approaches, providing methodologies to systematically evaluate algorithms for fairness. These tools act as magnifying glasses, revealing hidden biases in complex models and offering insights into addressing them.

Mitigating bias requires intentional strategies focused on fairness and equity, extending beyond technical interventions. It demands a shift in organisational practices and cultural mindsets. Regular audits of AI outcomes should become an integral part of company processes, ensuring continuous monitoring and improvement. Encouraging diverse leadership within tech companies can enhance the representation of varied perspectives, fostering inclusivity at every stage of AI development and implementation. By cultivating environments that embrace and promote equity and inclusion, organisations can nurture technological advances that reflect broader societal values.

Real-world cases highlight the urgency of addressing algorithmic bias. In healthcare, biased algorithms have led to unequal treatment recommendations for patients based on race or gender. A system trained primarily on data from one ethnic group might not accurately predict health outcomes for others, resulting in disparities in care Similarly, facial recognition technology has faced scrutiny for higher error rates among minority groups due to biased training data.

Overcoming these challenges requires a commitment to continuous improvement and vigilance. While AI holds immense promise, its impact depends on how it is developed and deployed. By prioritising fairness and inclusivity in AI design, we can create systems that reflect our highest societal values rather than perpetuating existing inequalities.

Reflection Section: Bias in Everyday Algorithms

Consider a time when you felt excluded or misrepresented by technology or a service. Reflect on potential biases contributing to that experience. How might inclusive data or design have changed your interaction?

The journey towards fairer AI is ongoing and requires collaboration across disciplines and communities. It involves embracing transparency in AI development to help users understand decision-making processes and hold systems accountable. Engaging with diverse stakeholders ensures multiple perspectives inform AI technologies' development, leading to robust and equitable solutions.

Addressing algorithmic bias remains a critical challenge as AI becomes an integral part of our lives. It's about building trust in the technologies we rely on daily and ensuring they work for everyone—not just a select few. Taking proactive steps toward fairness paves the way for an AI-driven future that benefits society holistically.

Responsible AI: Principles and Practices

Envision a world where AI systems thrive on fairness, transparency, and accountability. These principles underpin responsible AI, guiding its ethical development and deployment. Transparency involves open communication about how AI systems function and make decisions, ensuring users understand what happens behind the scenes. Accountability mandates that creators be held responsible for their systems' outcomes, preventing harm and upholding ethical standards. Fairness and inclusivity demand that AI serves everyone equally, preventing discrimination based on factors such as race or gender. These principles ensure AI benefits society while adhering to moral considerations.

Ethics committees play a pivotal role in overseeing AI projects, acting as guardians of these principles. They bring together multidisciplinary teams, including ethicists, technologists, and legal experts, to provide ethical oversight and ensure AI systems align with societal values. Regular reviews and updates of AI policies help adapt to emerging challenges and technologies. This proactive approach keeps ethics at the forefront of AI development, helping to prevent issues before they arise. Committees act as moral compasses, guiding organisations towards responsible AI practices that deliver societal benefits.

Real-world examples illustrate how organisations implement responsible AI measures. Many companies now publish ethical guidelines for their AI projects, outlining commitments to transparency, fairness, and accountability. These guidelines serve as public declarations of their ethical intentions, fostering user trust. Additionally, AI ethics training programmes equip developers with the knowledge and skills to create ethical systems, emphasising ethical implications throughout development.

Collaboration among stakeholders is crucial in promoting ethical AI practices. Partnerships with academia and non-profits provide valuable insights into ethical challenges and solutions. Diverse perspectives enrich discussions around ethical AI, while engaging end-users ensures their voices are considered in the development process. Involving users in ethics conversations helps create systems that meet their needs while respecting their rights. This collaborative approach fosters shared responsibility for ethical AI development.

Developing responsible AI requires a holistic approach, encompassing partnerships with academia to bridge knowledge gaps, collaboration with policymakers to craft inclusive legislation, and continuous public engagement to demystify AI's complexities.

This cross-sector collaboration ensures ethical guidelines evolve alongside technological advancements, fostering AI innovation that aligns with democratic values and societal benefits—ultimately making AI more inclusive and conscientious.

Interactive Element: Case Study Reflection

Reflect on a company you admire for its ethical stance on technology. How do they implement responsible AI practices and engage stakeholders in ethical discussions? What lessons can be gleaned from their approach?

The journey towards responsible AI is ongoing and requires the collective effort of all stakeholders. By adhering to core principles such as transparency, accountability, fairness, and inclusivity, we can create AI systems that serve society positively. Ethics committees provide essential oversight, ensuring these principles guide AI projects from inception to completion. Real-world examples illustrate organisations taking concrete steps towards responsible AI, setting a standard for others to emulate.

Collaboration is central to ethical AI development. Working with academia, non-profits, and end-users allows for a more effective resolution of ethical challenges and broader societal benefits. This approach fosters innovation while maintaining a strong moral foundation.

As we continue exploring AI's potential, prioritising ethics is crucial. Transparency, accountability, fairness, and inclusivity must remain at the heart of AI development to ensure technology remains a positive force in our increasingly digital world.

In this rapidly evolving landscape, ongoing education and adaptation are essential. Staying informed about emerging ethical challenges and evolving standards helps navigate AI complexities responsibly. Engaging in continuous learning and ethical discussions equips us to shape a future where AI benefits everyone equitably.

The path to responsible AI is not without challenges, but by embracing these principles and practices, we can create a future where technology serves humanity ethically and effectively. Let us work together to build a world where AI enhances our lives while respecting our values and rights.

Ethical Dilemmas in AI: Real-world Case Studies

AI isn't just about cutting-edge gadgets or algorithms crunching numbers; it's about navigating complex ethical dilemmas in real-world scenarios. Take facial recognition technology, for instance. Imagine walking down the street, unaware that cameras are identifying and tracking you. While this technology is powerful for security purposes, it raises significant privacy concerns, sparking debates about the acceptable limits of surveillance. The ethical challenge lies in balancing security with individual privacy rights—an ongoing societal tightrope.

Autonomous vehicles present another realm fraught with ethical dilemmas. These cars must make split-second decisions in critical situations. Imagine an autonomous vehicle facing an unavoidable accident—should it prioritise passenger safety or pedestrians? Such scenarios pose profound moral questions regarding machine decision-making in life-or-death situations. These dilemmas influence public perception and trust in AI. If people lack confidence in AI's ethical decision-making, they may resist its adoption, potentially hindering technological progress.

These ethical challenges shape policymaking and regulatory responses. Governments and organisations must develop frameworks that ensure AI operates fairly and transparently while safeguarding individual rights—all without stifling innovation. It is a delicate balancing act for policymakers: encouraging technological advancement while upholding ethical standards.

Transparency is crucial in addressing ethical dilemmas. Open communication about AI's limitations and risks is essential. When companies disclose how AI systems make decisions, they build trust with users. People want to understand how AI reaches its conclusions and why certain choices are made. Transparency demystifies AI, reassuring the public that no hidden agendas are at play.

Past case studies provide valuable insights into handling ethical challenges. Companies embroiled in ethical controversies often respond by establishing guidelines to prevent future issues. For example, after widespread concerns about facial recognition and privacy, some companies temporarily halted projects to assess their impact. By engaging with stakeholders and experts, they sought to develop more ethical deployment frameworks.

The ethical guidelines emerging from these experiences serve as roadmaps for navigating similar challenges. They highlight best practices and lessons, helping organisations avoid past mistakes. By studying how companies have addressed ethical dilemmas, we gain insights into designing AI systems that align with societal values.

Case studies reveal the complexity of AI ethics and the necessity of proactive engagement. Companies that cultivate a culture of responsibility involve diverse perspectives in decision-making, ensuring AI systems reflect a broad range of values and priorities.

Real-world examples remind us that ethical dilemmas are not abstract—they have tangible impacts on everyday life. Understanding these challenges equips us to develop AI technologies that genuinely benefit society. Prioritising transparency, engaging stakeholders, and adhering to ethical guidelines allow us to navigate AI ethics with confidence and integrity.

These case studies reshape our understanding of the evolving relationship between technology and ethics. As AI continues to transform our world, recognising its ethical implications empowers us to make informed choices about its use. By learning from real-world experiences, we can create a future where AI enhances our lives while respecting our values and rights.

Future-Proofing Ethics in AI Development

As AI evolves, new ethical challenges require anticipation and response. Imagine AI deeply embedded in surveillance systems, constantly monitoring public spaces. While such technology enhances security, it also poses significant threats to individual freedoms and privacy. Striking a balance between safety and personal rights is a pressing ethical concern as AI-driven surveillance expands.

In healthcare, AI promises precision diagnostics and personalised treatments, revolutionising patient care. However, ethical considerations around consent, data usage, and equitable access demand careful navigation. As AI assumes a greater role in medical decision-making, the potential for bias or errors in life-and-death situations raises profound moral dilemmas requiring urgent attention.

To address these emerging challenges, proactive ethical frameworks must evolve alongside AI innovation. Forward-thinking policies should guide AI research, embedding ethical considerations from the outset. This necessitates anticipatory governance models that enable flexible regulation, adapting as technology progresses. By foreseeing potential ethical issues, we can establish guidelines that prevent harm and promote responsible AI development. Ethical foresight encourages AI researchers to consider both individual and societal impacts of their work.

Continuous learning and adaptation are crucial to future-proofing AI ethics. As new challenges emerge, staying informed is essential. Ethics training for AI professionals equips them to navigate complex moral landscapes. Keeping pace with evolving ethical standards ensures AI practitioners remain vigilant about new developments. Ongoing education fosters a culture of responsibility within the AI community, empowering individuals to act as ethical stewards of technology.

Innovation must align with ethical foresight, ensuring technological advancements reflect societal values. Integrating ethical considerations into AI research and development prioritises responsibility alongside innovation. Striking a balance between pushing technological boundaries and fulfilling moral obligations is vital. Open dialogue with stakeholders—including policymakers, ethicists, and the public—ensures diverse perspectives inform AI development. Collaboration with these groups helps identify potential risks early and devise effective mitigation strategies.

As we look to AI's future, fostering an environment that encourages both innovation and ethical responsibility is paramount. A mindset that values technological progress while upholding fundamental rights will lead to AI systems that enhance human capabilities without compromising ethical standards.

In summary, future-proofing AI ethics requires a proactive approach, anticipating emerging challenges and adapting to new realities. By establishing flexible frameworks, prioritising continuous learning, and embracing ethical foresight, we can navigate AI ethics with confidence and integrity. Responsible innovation ensures AI serves humanity, improving lives while respecting values and freedoms.

Looking ahead, we will explore how AI is transforming various industries, from healthcare to finance. We will examine the profound impact of AI-driven innovation and the opportunities it presents for growth and advancement. Stay tuned as we delve into the dynamic world of AI and its ever-evolving influence on society.

Chapter 7

Future Trends and Emerging Technologies

AI and the Internet of Things (IoT): A Connected Future

Picture a bustling city where traffic lights adjust dynamically to ease congestion or a farm where sensors monitor soil moisture to ensure optimal crop growth. This is not a distant fantasy but the rapidly emerging world of AI and IoT. When artificial intelligence merges with the Internet of Things, it creates a network of smarter, more responsive environments. These interconnected systems enable devices to communicate, analyse data, and make autonomous decisions that enhance daily life.

Smart cities exemplify this transformation, using AI to manage traffic flow efficiently, reducing commute times and lowering emissions. Imagine your car receiving real-time updates on the best routes, saving time and reducing stress. In agriculture, AI-enhanced IoT devices collect data on weather patterns, soil conditions, and crop health, enabling precision farming that maximises yield while minimising resource use.

Beyond traffic management, IoT networks in smart cities can revolutionise urban living. Imagine streetlights that automatically dim or brighten depending on pedestrian or vehicular movement, conserving energy without compromising safety. Smart waste bins equipped with sensors could notify collection teams when they are full, optimising routes and reducing unnecessary labour. Similarly, AI-driven water management systems can detect leaks and inefficiencies, helping municipalities conserve water and reduce losses. These examples illustrate how AI and IoT are reshaping the infrastructure of modern cities.

The sheer volume of data generated by IoT devices is staggering. Consider a single smart home, where thermostats, security cameras, and kitchen appliances continuously collect data. Without AI, this information would be like an unorganised library—vast but impractical. AI processes these datasets in real-time, enabling devices to make instant, informed decisions. In industrial settings, this translates into predictive maintenance, allowing machines to anticipate and address potential failures before they occur, reducing downtime and saving costs. Likewise, smart energy grids use AI to manage consumption dynamically, preventing outages during peak demand.

This impact extends to healthcare, where AI and IoT can revolutionise patient monitoring. Wearable devices can track vital signs and relay data to healthcare providers in real-time, enabling early detection of health issues and improving patient outcomes. For instance, continuous glucose monitors for diabetics can automatically adjust insulin pumps, maintaining optimal glucose levels without manual intervention. Such innovations demonstrate AI and IoT's potential to transform industries and improve lives fundamentally.

However, these advancements come with challenges. Integrating AI with IoT raises significant security concerns. Connected devices can become entry points for cyber-attacks if not adequately secured. Imagine a hacker gaining control of a home's heating system or accessing personal data via a smart speaker. The need for robust cybersecurity is paramount, as vulnerabilities in connected home devices could lead to privacy breaches. AI-driven security protocols are being developed to monitor networks for suspicious activity and respond swiftly to threats, offering a layer of protection against potential cyber risks.

Beyond urban and industrial applications, AI and IoT are transforming other sectors. In hospitality, AI-enabled IoT devices personalise guest experiences, adjusting room settings to match preferences upon check-in. In retail, AI optimises inventory management and enhances customer engagement through adaptive store layouts and tailored promotions. Even the entertainment industry benefits, with AI dynamically adjusting audio-visual settings to match user preferences or moods, creating a more immersive experience.

Looking to the future, the integration of AI and IoT promises even more ground-breaking applications. In healthcare, AI-assisted monitoring devices could track patients' vital signs in real-time, alerting medical professionals to anomalies requiring urgent attention. This proactive approach could revolutionise patient care by identifying potential health risks before they become severe. In logistics, autonomous drones equipped with IoT sensors could deliver packages efficiently, bypassing traffic altogether. Environmental monitoring systems could leverage AI and IoT to track pollution levels and climate changes, providing critical insights for sustainability initiatives and policy-making.

AI and IoT also hold immense potential in disaster management. Using predictive analytics, AI can interpret data from IoT sensors deployed in disaster-prone areas. Early warning systems powered by these technologies could alert communities to impending threats such as earthquakes, floods, or hurricanes, enabling timely evacuations and resource allocation. This integration could save lives and minimise property damage.

Moreover, AI and IoT can redefine education through smart campus innovations. Universities can implement AI-powered lecture capture systems that provide personalised feedback, while IoT-enabled learning environments foster interactive and immersive experiences. AI-driven infrastructure management can optimise energy use, enhancing sustainability efforts in educational institutions.

As AI and IoT continue to evolve, their convergence offers unprecedented opportunities across industries. The challenge lies in harnessing their full potential while addressing security, privacy, and ethical concerns. By ensuring responsible innovation, we can create intelligent, efficient, and sustainable systems that enhance quality of life while safeguarding individual rights and societal values.

Reflection Section

Consider how AI and IoT have already influenced your environment. Which devices in your life utilise these technologies? Reflect on the

potential improvements these innovations bring to your daily experiences.
As AI and IoT continue to evolve, the future holds endless possibilities. Their dynamics will enhance everyday conveniences and transform entire industries, redefining how we interact with the world around us. As these technologies advance, they will undoubtedly open new avenues for innovation and exploration, inviting us all to rethink what is possible.

Cloud Computing and AI: A Synergistic Relationship

Imagine a world where every small business and startup can access cutting-edge AI technologies without needing a room full of servers. This is the magic of cloud computing, which democratises AI by offering platforms like Google Cloud AI. These platforms provide machine learning tools that anyone can use to train models or analyse data. Before cloud computing, such resources were only available to tech giants with deep pockets. Now, even a small team with a big idea can leverage these tools to innovate and compete globally. The cloud makes AI accessible, opening doors for creativity and disruption that we hadn't thought possible.

To better understand the democratising effect of cloud computing, consider the educational sector. Universities and schools can now use cloud AI to offer machine learning courses without heavy investments in infrastructure. Students from varied backgrounds gain access to rich resources and knowledge, preparing them for future tech-related fields. Remote learning has also benefited, with AI-driven platforms facilitating personalised and adaptive learning experiences for students globally. The cloud thus acts as an indispensable resource, levelling the playing field across education and emphasising skills over mere access to technology.

The beauty of cloud-based AI services lies in their scalability. Need more computing power? The cloud can expand to meet your demands without breaking a sweat. This flexibility is a game-changer for startups that can't afford to invest heavily in infrastructure right away. They can start small and scale up as they grow, only paying for what they use. It's like renting an office space that grows with your company; rather than buying a huge building you'll only fill years down the line. This approach reduces overhead costs significantly, allowing businesses to allocate resources more efficiently and focus on innovation rather than infrastructure.

Beyond just hosting AI workloads, integrating AI into cloud services is creating more intelligent and efficient solutions. Think about cloud storage—traditionally, it has been about saving files and data securely. Now, with AI in the mix, these systems can optimise storage space automatically, archiving less-used data to free up room for what you need most. Intelligent resource management goes further by predicting usage patterns and adjusting capacities in real time, ensuring that services run smoothly without unnecessary downtime or wasted resources. This proactive management means you always have what you need when you need it, without lifting a finger.

Imagine cloud computing, through AI, playing a pivotal role in healthcare. Cloud services securely store vast amounts of medical data, while AI analyses it to predict patient trends, disease outbreaks, or potential health risks. This fusion allows for more accurate diagnostics and personalised care plans. Hospitals and clinics, particularly in rural or underserved areas, can access resources that were once beyond their reach, leading to improved healthcare delivery and outcomes.

Looking to the future, the possibilities of cloud-AI integration are nothing short of exciting. Edge computing is poised to take real-time data processing to the next level by moving some of the computational load closer to the data source. Imagine a self-driving car processing its environment instantly without relying solely on distant cloud servers. This advancement could revolutionise industries that require immediate decision-making capabilities. Moreover, AI-driven security enhancements are expected to bolster cloud environments against cyber threats, offering more robust protection through continuous learning and adaptation to emerging threats.

In addition to business applications, cloud-AI dynamics are making waves in education and research. Virtual classrooms powered by cloud-based AI can provide students with personalised learning experiences that adapt to their unique pace and understanding.

Research institutions benefit from the massive computational power for complex simulations and data analysis, accelerating scientific discoveries across various fields.

But what does all this mean for you? Well, it means that as these technologies advance, they become more integrated into everyday experiences, often without you even realising it. Your favourite apps running smoothly on your phone or the seamless streaming of your favourite shows are all thanks to these invisible tech advancements working tirelessly in the background. As businesses and developers continue to push the boundaries of what's possible with cloud and AI, we can expect even more innovative solutions that make life easier, more efficient, and even more fun.

Moreover, cloud-based AI can foster innovation in fields such as environmental conservation and smart agriculture. By analysing climatic data patterns, AI could significantly shift agricultural practices towards increased sustainability and resource efficiency. For instance, AI could optimise crop rotation schedules according to predicted rainfall and temperature changes, maximising yield with minimal environmental impact. Similarly, wildlife conservation efforts could benefit from AI-powered predictive models, offering early insights into ecological disruptions and enabling proactive measures to protect biodiversity.

Cloud computing and AI are headed for bright futures, with each pushing the other toward greater heights. As they evolve together, they'll undoubtedly unlock new opportunities for growth and creativity across various sectors. From healthcare to entertainment, education to finance, this dynamic duo promises to continue transforming our world in ways we're only beginning to understand.

The Rise of AI in Cybersecurity

Picture a digital fortress, tirelessly patrolling its walls for invisible invaders. This is the role of AI in cybersecurity today. As cyber threats become more sophisticated, AI emerges as a potent ally, enhancing our ability to defend against these evolving challenges. AI-powered threat detection systems are akin to vigilant guards, analysing patterns and sifting through massive data streams to identify potential threats before they manifest. Imagine a security camera that not only films but also predicts suspicious activities before they happen. By employing machine learning, these systems learn from past incidents, spotting anomalies in network traffic that might indicate a breach. This proactive approach turns the tables on cybercriminals, who find themselves outpaced by the speed and accuracy of AI defences.

To delve deeper into the practicalities of AI in cybersecurity, consider a corporate environment where AI systems monitor employee activities to identify unusual patterns that might suggest insider threats. These intelligent systems perceive more than just direct attacks, anticipating cyber intruders' subtle manoeuvres and proactively preventing data breaches. Predictive analytics also plays a significant role, using historical data to forecast potential vulnerabilities. This foresight grants cybersecurity teams the upper hand to counteract threats before they rear their heads, maintaining the integrity and trustworthiness of organisational data.

Predictive capabilities are where AI truly shines. Think of it as having a crystal ball that forewarns of cyber threats lurking on the horizon. Predictive modelling allows AI to forecast potential attacks by analysing historical data and identifying trends. This foresight enables organisations to implement defensive measures in advance, nipping attacks in the bud. Risk assessment tools powered by AI evaluate vulnerabilities within systems, suggesting fortifications where needed. It's like having a digital strategist constantly evaluating your defences and advising on the best ways to fortify them against future incursions.

In tandem with AI-driven defences, companies are devising more sophisticated encryption methodologies bolstered by AI to safeguard sensitive data. Machine learning algorithms optimise encryption processes, ensuring that data remains secure yet accessible to legitimate users. Furthermore, AI enhances incident response strategies, streamlining recovery procedures post-attack. Automated AI systems can quickly analyse the aftermath of a breach, reducing downtime and swiftly restoring normalcy.

However, relying on AI for cybersecurity isn't without its challenges. One significant concern is adversarial attacks, where attackers attempt to trick AI systems by feeding them misleading data. It's like trying to confuse a guard dog with a scent trail leading the wrong way. Ensuring AI transparency and accountability is another hurdle. Users need confidence that these systems operate fairly and without bias, especially when they play such a crucial role in protection. Trust is paramount when machines handle sensitive data that could affect both privacy and security.

AI technologies are further transforming identity management and authentication processes. Think of a world where passwords are obsolete, replaced by more secure biometric verification methods powered by AI. These systems could utilise facial recognition, retina scans, or voice patterns, making unauthorised access significantly more difficult. Companies are investing in AI to develop these sophisticated identity verification methods, thereby enhancing the security of both digital and physical spaces.

Looking ahead, the role of AI in shaping cybersecurity strategies is bound to expand. Imagine identity verification processes enhanced by AI, where your digital ID is as secure as your fingerprint. These systems could revolutionise how we verify identities online, making it harder for malicious actors to impersonate legitimate users. Autonomous security systems are another promising development. Imagine an AI system autonomously identifying and mitigating threats in real-time without human intervention. Such systems could act swiftly to neutralise attacks, reducing response times from minutes to mere milliseconds.

This exciting evolution doesn't stop there. Imagine governments integrating AI into national cybersecurity infrastructures, using AI's pattern recognition capabilities to protect a nation's critical infrastructure, financial institutions, and communication networks from sophisticated cyber threats. AI-backed intelligence can continuously monitor geopolitical cyber tensions and respond proactively to mitigate risks.

Furthermore, AI fosters more seamless integration of prevention strategies across global networks. Through multinational collaborations, AI frameworks could share real-time threat intelligence, empowering nations and organisations to stay ahead of impending dangers. This collective cybersecurity network would create a formidable defence where the sharing of AI-driven insights leads to heightened global security resilience.

AI's influence on cybersecurity is undeniable, offering tools and strategies that keep us one step ahead of cyber threats. As technology evolves, so do the tactics employed by cybercriminals. However, with AI's predictive prowess and ongoing advancements in automation and security protocols, there's hope for a safer digital realm. It's an exciting time for cybersecurity, with AI playing a central role in defining how we protect our digital lives and assets from ever-present threats.

AI in Autonomous Vehicles: Steering Towards the Future

Imagine cruising down the highway, hands off the wheel, as your car effortlessly navigates traffic. This is the world of autonomous vehicles, where AI is the driving force behind this groundbreaking technology. At the heart of these vehicles are sophisticated AI algorithms that enable real-time navigation and obstacle detection. These systems scan the environment, identifying everything from pedestrians to unpredictable road conditions, allowing the vehicle to make split-second decisions. It's like having a digital co-pilot with eyes everywhere, ensuring a safe journey from point A to B. Machine learning plays a crucial role here, too, constantly updating the vehicle's knowledge base for predictive maintenance and diagnostics. This means your car can anticipate issues before they become problems, saving time and reducing the need for unexpected repairs.

Consider the cutting-edge collaborations between automotive companies and tech giants aimed at enhancing the sensory inputs of autonomous cars. By integrating state-of-the-art LiDAR systems, cameras, and radar, these vehicles gain enhanced environmental awareness, paving the way for more sophisticated decision-making capabilities. Test tracks worldwide simulate complex driving scenarios, teaching AI systems to navigate challenges from heavy traffic to adverse weather, ultimately improving reliability and safety.

The road to autonomy, however, isn't just about technology—it's a complex landscape filled with safety and regulatory considerations. Ethical decision-making in driving scenarios becomes increasingly critical as these vehicles become more common. Picture a situation where an autonomous car must choose between two unfavourable outcomes—how should it decide? Such dilemmas demand careful thought and robust ethical frameworks to guide AI systems in making choices that align with societal values. Regulatory bodies worldwide work tirelessly to establish guidelines for deploying these vehicles, ensuring they meet safety standards and operate within legal boundaries.

Beyond regulation, public acceptance plays a significant role in the widespread adoption of autonomous vehicles. Public education campaigns are crucial in dispelling myths and fears about relinquishing control to machines on the road. Cultural acceptance, therefore, hinges on consistent transparency about the technologies used, safety records, and the tangible benefits these vehicles offer in daily commutes.

Real-world deployments of autonomous vehicles are already reshaping transportation landscapes. In some cities, AI-driven public transportation systems are revolutionising how people commute. Buses and shuttles equipped with autonomous technology provide reliable and efficient service without human drivers. Similarly, autonomous delivery vehicles are becoming a familiar sight in urban environments, zipping around to deliver goods quickly and efficiently. These innovations help reduce traffic congestion and emissions while offering convenient solutions for last-mile delivery challenges.

Educational institutions are also jumping on the bandwagon, incorporating autonomous technology into their research and development. Universities partner with tech companies to create courses focused on autonomous vehicle technology, preparing the next generation of engineers to further this exciting field. By fostering interdisciplinary collaboration, these programs are incubating future innovations that will drive the technology further into the mainstream.

Economic implications are equally notable. Autonomous vehicles are poised to transform industries reliant on transportation, from logistics to ride-hailing. Businesses will be drawn to the potential for reduced operational costs and increased efficiency. Additionally, this technology could open new career avenues, as skilled professionals will be required to maintain, program, and oversee the continuous development of autonomous systems.

Looking to the horizon, the future of autonomous vehicles promises even greater advancements. Level 5 autonomy—the point where vehicles require no human intervention—holds immense potential to transform society. Imagine a world where you can relax or work during your commute without ever needing to take the wheel. This level of autonomy will also enable seamless vehicle-to-infrastructure communication, where cars interact with traffic signals, road sensors, and other infrastructure elements to optimise traffic flow and enhance safety. Such integration could dramatically reduce accidents and improve urban mobility.

Research continues to explore the societal impacts of widespread autonomous vehicle adoption. By studying changes in mobility patterns, urban planning, and environmental policy, we can prepare for and adapt to the shifts these vehicles induce. Predictive analytics help forecast future transportation needs, enabling cities to design infrastructure that accommodates autonomous technology while ensuring equitable access for all communities.

Further advancements could see autonomous vehicles supporting emergency response and public safety. AI-driven vehicles might assist in providing timely aid during natural disasters or emergencies, acting as transport for first responders or as mobile units that deliver medical supplies and equipment to affected areas efficiently.

The journey toward fully autonomous vehicles continues to captivate innovators and consumers alike, offering a glimpse into a future where driving as we know it may become a thing of the past. As these technologies advance, they will reshape not only how we travel but also how we plan our cities and live our lives. The possibilities are vast and exciting, promising a world where convenience, safety, and efficiency go hand in hand.

Reflection Section

Think about how autonomous vehicles might change your daily routine in the future. Would you welcome the idea of a car that drives itself? Reflect on how this technology could impact your lifestyle and transportation choices as it evolves.

Moreover, broader implications in terms of environmental benefits should be considered. Autonomous vehicles, particularly electricity-powered, could drastically reduce carbon footprints, aiding efforts toward more sustainable urban environments.

The evolution of autonomous vehicles is an exciting frontier where AI meets real-world challenges head-on. With each milestone achieved, we move closer to a future where cars drive themselves seamlessly through complex urban environments, offering unparalleled convenience and safety.

Predicting AI's Next Big Trends

Imagine a world where AI works hand in hand with quantum computing, unlocking possibilities once thought impossible. This isn't science fiction—it's a burgeoning reality. Quantum computing, with its staggering ability to process information at unprecedented speeds, is set to revolutionize industries alongside AI. By solving complex problems that stump even today's supercomputers, AI-driven quantum advancements could lead to breakthroughs in everything from drug discovery to climate modeling. It's like upgrading from a bicycle to a spaceship—the leap in capability is that vast.

Another exciting frontier is neuromorphic computing, which mimics the human brain's structure to enhance AI's processing power. This technology could transform how we approach tasks like pattern recognition and sensory processing. Imagine a computer that learns and adapts just like a human, offering rapid and nuanced insights. The possibilities are immense, from developing more intuitive personal assistants to crafting advanced robotics with human-like cognition.

AI is also driving significant advancements in natural language processing (NLP). Future NLP systems, powered by cutting-edge AI models, could enable seamless communication between humans and machines, transcending language barriers globally. Real-time, highly accurate translation that preserves cultural nuances is edging closer, fostering understanding and collaboration on an unprecedented scale.

As AI's capabilities expand, it intersects with other fields in transformative ways. In biotechnology, AI is paving the way for personalised medicine tailored to an individual's genetic makeup. Imagine treatments designed specifically for you—more effective, with fewer side effects. AI models analyse genetic data to predict how patients might respond to different therapies, shifting healthcare from a one-size-fits-all approach to a more customized experience. In materials science, AI accelerates the discovery of new compounds, leading to innovations in stronger, lighter structures and more efficient energy storage solutions.

Breakthroughs in energy technology are also on the horizon, with AI optimizing renewable energy sources. Smart grids, powered by AI, can efficiently distribute solar and wind energy based on demand, minimizing waste and maximizing sustainability. Predictive analytics could forecast energy usage patterns, further enhancing conservation efforts and supporting a global shift towards greener power solutions.

Furthermore, AI's integration with augmented reality (AR) and virtual reality (VR) is blurring the lines between the physical and digital worlds. Imagine immersive experiences that adapt in real-time to human emotions and contexts, revolutionizing entertainment, education, and healthcare. Virtual classrooms could tailor lessons to individual learning speeds, while immersive VR therapies could aid in mental health treatments.

These advancements will have profound effects on the workforce. As AI evolves, it reshapes the skills required across various professions. Just as the internet created jobs unimaginable a few decades ago, AI is generating new opportunities while transforming existing roles. The demand for AI proficiency is rising, pushing professionals to adapt by learning new skills and embracing continuous education. But rather than simply replacing jobs, AI can free humans from repetitive tasks, allowing them to focus on creative problem-solving and innovation. This shift could lead to more fulfilling careers where technology complements human ingenuity.

Organizations are already investing in training programs to build AI competency among employees, anticipating future workplace demands. By embracing lifelong learning, professionals can stay relevant and actively participate in shaping the technological landscape.

Amidst these rapid advancements, ethical considerations remain paramount. As AI becomes more integrated into decision-making, ensuring its responsible use is crucial. Proactive governance is needed to manage emerging technologies ethically and transparently. This includes addressing bias in AI systems, ensuring algorithmic transparency, and maintaining accountability for AI-driven outcomes.

Innovative partnerships between technology companies and regulatory bodies are working to anticipate ethical challenges, fostering environments where AI thrives responsibly. Public discourse also plays a key role in shaping policies that balance innovation with societal well-being.

Moreover, global collaboration in setting universal AI guidelines will be essential in managing its influence. By harmonizing efforts across nations, we can ensure that AI serves humanity's best interests, providing equitable benefits while mitigating potential risks.

As we close this chapter, it's clear that AI's future is both exhilarating and complex. Its vast potential must be matched with thoughtful management and ethical foresight. In the next chapter, we'll explore how these advancements intersect with industries like healthcare and education, shaping both technology and our everyday lives. Stay tuned as we delve into the broader implications of this technological evolution and its impact on society.

Chapter 8

Empowering Careers with AI

Upskilling with AI: Career Advancement Strategies

Imagine standing at the crossroads of your career, contemplating the vast possibilities ahead. In this transformative era, AI is not just an emerging trend but a powerful ally reshaping career trajectories across diverse fields. No longer a niche concept reserved for tech enthusiasts, AI has become an essential tool influencing industries worldwide. The key challenge now is identifying which AI competencies are gaining prominence and how they can propel your career forward.

One of the most sought-after skills today is **data analysis and interpretation**, much like a detective piecing together clues to uncover a hidden truth. In a world overflowing with data, companies are eager to find professionals who can navigate vast information reserves and extract meaningful insights. Context is everything—the ability to connect data points leads to a deeper understanding of consumer behavior, operational efficiencies, and market trends that might otherwise remain obscured.

Machine learning expertise is another indispensable skill forming the backbone of AI. These algorithms empower systems to learn autonomously and improve over time. While deep programming expertise isn't necessary, a foundational understanding of how machine learning models work and their practical applications can be invaluable. For instance, predictive algorithms in marketing help forecast customer behavior, enabling businesses to craft more targeted strategies. Similarly, in healthcare, AI-driven diagnostics are revolutionizing early disease detection and preventive care.

AI literacy is no longer optional—it's becoming essential across all levels of an organization. From sales forecasting to supply chain optimization, AI is embedded in business operations and decision-making processes. Professionals with AI knowledge can make strategic contributions that enhance efficiency and innovation. Imagine a project manager who understands AI—by leveraging predictive analytics, they can refine project timelines, optimize resource allocation, and mitigate risks with remarkable accuracy. Such expertise fosters agility within teams and increases project success rates.

To stay ahead, professionals must adopt a **personalised learning path** aligned with their career ambitions. Fortunately, today's educational landscape is more accessible than ever. Online platforms like Coursera, edX, and Udacity offer specialized courses that cater to various industries, whether in finance, healthcare, or the creative arts. Additionally, industry-specific workshops and seminars provide valuable insights into AI's evolving role while creating opportunities for networking with like-minded professionals.

Mentorship is a crucial pillar of the AI upskilling journey. Finding a mentor can be like uncovering a hidden passage in a complex maze. Platforms like LinkedIn provide access to industry leaders willing to share their expertise. AI-focused mentorship programs offer invaluable guidance, exposing learners to real-world challenges and insider knowledge. Mentors don't just impart technical skills—they offer career advice, boost confidence, and help expand professional networks. Many success stories highlight how mentorship has been a catalyst for growth, helping individuals transition smoothly into AI-driven roles.

Beyond learning, **practical experience is essential** in mastering AI. While theoretical knowledge lays the foundation, hands-on experience cements understanding. Engaging in open-source AI projects allows individuals to experiment with real-world applications, gaining insights into the tangible impact of AI solutions. Developing personal projects that address meaningful challenges nurtures problem-solving skills and creativity. Maintaining an online portfolio to document these projects can serve as a powerful testament to expertise, making a strong impression on potential employers.

In this rapidly evolving era, AI proficiency is more than just a competitive edge—it's becoming a necessity. By acquiring relevant skills, seeking mentorship, and engaging in hands-on projects, professionals can confidently navigate the AI-driven job market and unlock new opportunities. The future belongs to those who embrace AI, adapt to change, and continuously evolve alongside technological advancements.

Interactive Element: Reflection Section

Pause momentarily and write down three AI skills you aim to develop, considering your professional aspirations. Identify potential resources or mentors from whom to seek advice in mastering these skills.

By embracing these strategies, you're not merely advancing your career but establishing yourself as an indispensable figure in your chosen industry. The journey into AI may initially seem daunting, but with tailored skills, mentorship, and hands-on practice, it transforms into an exhilarating voyage filled with limitless growth potential and innovative discoveries. The course you chart with AI is not merely about the technology but about how it transforms you into an influential leader in tomorrow's workforce.

Navigating AI Tools for Professional Growth

Imagine standing before a vast toolbox, where each compartment presents a variety of possibilities to propel your career forward. AI tools fill these compartments, offering diverse avenues for amplifying productivity and creativity. Among them, TensorFlow and PyTorch stand out as quintessential platforms for machine learning, facilitating the building of models that evolve with data and progressively enhance accuracy. Whether your goal is to optimize algorithms or predict market trends, these tools serve as invaluable allies. Tableau is highly favored by those captivated by transforming raw data into compelling narratives. Its intuitive drag-and-drop interface enables the creation of interactive charts and dashboards, making intricate data accessible to all. These tools don't just simplify tasks—they unlock new dimensions of innovation and discovery.

Beyond the most popular AI tools, consider exploring lesser-known platforms like KNIME for advanced data analytics and Microsoft's Power BI for integrating sophisticated data analysis into daily operations. These platforms offer unique features tailored to diverse business needs and can sometimes provide more seamless integration than widely known solutions. Furthermore, tools like RapidMiner offer intuitive platforms for conducting advanced analytics and predictive modeling, significantly expanding data analysis capabilities.

Incorporating AI tools into your everyday routine is akin to discovering a faster route to work—it saves time, boosts efficiency, and makes life significantly easier. Take AI-enhanced project management tools, for example. These streamline workflows, automating mundane tasks such as scheduling and task allocation, allowing you to focus on essential endeavors—creative problem-solving and strategic formulation. By automating repetitive activities through AI-driven systems, you free up valuable time and cognitive resources for innovation. Imagine a workplace where mundane data entry is seamlessly handled by AI, enabling brainstorming for the next groundbreaking idea or refining intricate strategies. This integration revolutionizes both individual productivity and team dynamics, fostering a more collaborative and efficient environment.

AI tools are becoming increasingly indispensable across various industries. In finance, AI plays a critical role in risk assessment and financial analysis, with algorithms meticulously processing extensive datasets to identify potential risks and opportunities, thereby enabling informed decision-making. In marketing, AI-driven platforms automate processes ranging from customer segmentation to personalised content delivery, enhancing engagement and return on investment. Imagine marketing strategies that adapt in real time, responding to consumer behavior insights—AI facilitates such advancements. Across industries, leveraging AI tools for these applications positions businesses more competitively, making them nimble and adaptable.

Keeping up with evolving AI tools and technologies is akin to regularly updating your vehicle's navigation system—you continuously know the optimal path to take. Subscribe to newsletters from leading AI platforms to stay informed about the latest features and innovations. Attending webinars and conferences immerses you in emerging trends and best practices. These gatherings aren't just educational opportunities but also goldmines for networking, where you can connect with like-minded professionals and industry leaders. Continuous learning isn't just about keeping pace—it's about ensuring you remain at the cutting edge in a world where change is constant.

Interactive Element: Case Study

Examine how a small startup seamlessly integrated AI tools into their daily routines, achieving a remarkable 30% efficiency boost and significant operational cost reduction.

AI's beauty lies in its adaptability and potential to redefine career possibilities. By embracing these tools and weaving them into professional endeavors, you enhance efficiency and forge pathways for innovation and expansive growth. Whether automating routine tasks or developing complex models, AI offers numerous methods to refine skills and broaden horizons. It's an exhilarating time to be at the front of this technological wave, where each tool represents a new opportunity waiting to be explored.

AI Certification and Learning Resources

Visualize this scenario: you're mingling at a networking event, engaging with a hiring manager intrigued by your resume. They inquire about your AI experience. You mention the certifications you've obtained, and suddenly, you're not just another applicant—you're the candidate with verified expertise. AI certifications can be the key differentiator in today's fiercely competitive job market. They serve as a seal of authenticity on your skill set, certifying your ability to tackle AI challenges. Recognized industry certifications not only enhance your resume but also significantly boost your career prospects. They signal to employers your commitment to professional development, giving you an edge over those who claim AI knowledge without formal credentials.

Numerous esteemed AI certification programs are available, catering to diverse interests and proficiency levels. For those engrossed in machine learning, the Google AI Certification offers a comprehensive curriculum on model building and algorithm understanding. Alternatively, the IBM Data Science Professional Certificate immerses learners in data analysis, providing a robust foundation in handling and interpreting extensive datasets. These programs equip you with both theoretical knowledge and practical applications, ensuring a seamless transfer of learning to a professional environment.

Moreover, universities worldwide are incorporating AI into their curriculums, recognizing its crucial role in today's job market. Established institutions such as Stanford and MIT offer extensive programs in AI and related fields, providing comprehensive knowledge while introducing you to a network of professionals and experts in the community.

However, the pursuit of knowledge extends beyond certifications. A vast repository of resources awaits the intrepid explorer eager to dive deeper into AI. Massive Open Online Courses (MOOCs) such as Coursera and edX offer a broad spectrum of AI courses, covering fundamental concepts to advanced techniques. They provide flexibility, allowing you to learn at your own pace and convenience. Books and workshops also form an integral part of this learning ecosystem, offering diverse insights and perspectives. Attending AI-driven meetups and community events expands your network while exposing you to real-world applications and challenges encountered by seasoned professionals.

Selecting the right certification program can feel like standing at a crossroads with innumerable paths ahead. To choose wisely, evaluate the program content and its relevance to your career goals. Does the curriculum align with the skills needed to advance in your current role or pivot to a new one? Consider the time commitment required—can you manage it alongside your current responsibilities? Also, assess the financial investment involved. While some programs require significant upfront costs, their returns can be substantial in career growth and potential salary increments. Weigh these factors carefully to ensure the path you choose aligns with both your professional aspirations and personal circumstances.

Visual Element: Resource List

Craft a detailed list of online platforms offering AI courses, encompassing pros and cons, to aid you in deciding where to commence your learning journey.

Investing in AI certifications and learning resources illustrates a steadfast commitment to continuous evolution and adaptation in an ever-changing field. These credentials unlock doors to new opportunities, equipping you with the confidence to navigate complex challenges effectively. As you amplify your skillset through these avenues, you'll find yourself not only keeping pace with industry advancements but distinguishing yourself as a coveted professional poised to embrace the future of AI.

Communicating AI Concepts to Non-Technical Teams

Picture yourself presenting at a team meeting, where colleagues unfamiliar with AI jargon listen somewhat perplexed as you explain the latest AI initiative. This scenario highlights why mastering effective communication is crucial in bridging the gap between technical and non-technical teams. Simplifying the language makes AI concepts accessible—replacing algorithmic complexities with straightforward explanations can make all the difference. Instead of delving into computational intricacies, compare a neural network to a web of connections, akin to a human brain processing inputs and identifying patterns. Contextual analogies demystify technology, making it more approachable to those unversed in data science.

Utilizing analogies is a powerful strategy. Imagine explaining machine learning as akin to training a dog to perform new tricks. The dog learns skills and improves its performance through repetition and rewards (or data)—a parallel to how AI systems learn from data, enhancing predictions and achieving greater accuracy. Analogies like these encapsulate complex processes, making them digestible without overwhelming the audience with technical jargon.

Fostering cross-functional collaboration requires more than just understanding—it demands teamwork. Recurring meetings between AI specialists and non-specialists create an environment where ideas converge. By discussing shared goals and aspirations, teams unify under a single vision. Establishing what each team aims to achieve aligns efforts, propelling everyone toward the same target. This collaborative spirit fosters trust and drives innovation, nurturing a workplace where transformative ideas can flourish.

Visual aids and storytelling are instrumental in communicating complex ideas effectively. Visuals provide a concise snapshot of processes, with infographics detailing AI workflows to facilitate quick comprehension at a glance. They succinctly depict data flows and system operations, shaping a clearer image of AI's integration into existing structures. Additionally, storytelling breathes life into AI implementations through case studies showcasing successful AI-driven projects that address tangible challenges. These narratives underscore AI's potential, elucidating its benefits in practical settings.

Common misunderstandings about AI often stem from misconceptions or uncertainties. To address these misunderstandings, clarify AI's role as a tool that augments human abilities rather than supplanting them. Emphasize that AI excels at handling mundane tasks, freeing humans to focus on strategic decisions and creative problem-solving. Reframing AI as a complement to human skills alleviates concerns about job displacement, highlighting its supportive rather than competitive nature.

Address objections with empathy and factual evidence. To mitigate concerns about losing control over automated systems, illustrate how AI is designed with fail-safes and human oversight to ensure responsible application. Highlight instances where AI has enriched job roles, boosting efficiency and productivity while retaining essential human involvement.

Textual Element: Reflection Section

Recall a moment when you had to explain a complex subject to someone outside your expertise. How did you simplify it? Reflect on the practical strategies and think about how they could be applied when discussing AI with non-technical teams.

Effective communication of AI concepts demands empathy, patience, and creativity. You bridge the chasm between technical complexities and lay understanding by demystifying technical jargon, harnessing relatable analogies, encouraging collaboration, employing visuals, and empathetically addressing misunderstandings. This approach harmonizes team dynamics and empowers everyone to leverage AI's potential collaboratively and confidently.

Building an AI-Ready Resume

Creating an AI-ready resume resembles assembling a puzzle where every piece must fit perfectly. Showcasing your key AI competencies is paramount. Think of it as an engaging narrative about your AI journey—what projects have you undertaken? What achievements make you proud? Highlight these prominently. Have you developed a chatbot that improved customer engagement or crafted a machine-learning model that enhanced sales forecasts? These experiences demonstrate your ability to apply AI concepts practically. Additionally, they emphasize your technical proficiency with AI tools. Whether using TensorFlow, PyTorch, or conducting data visualization with platforms like Tableau, these skills form the core of your AI toolkit, proving your readiness to translate theoretical knowledge into real-world applications.

Customizing your resume for specific AI roles is like a chef tailoring a recipe for different tastes—each opportunity demands a unique touch. Start by aligning your resume content with job descriptions, incorporating relevant keywords and phrases. This strategy ensures your resume passes initial screenings. Highlight transferable skills relevant to AI roles, even if they originate from seemingly unrelated fields. Problem-solving, analytical thinking, and collaboration are especially valued in AI-driven environments. They showcase adaptability and resilience in a rapidly evolving field.

AI certifications and education serve as prestigious accolades on your resume. Highlight any AI courses and certifications you've completed. Whether it's Google's AI Certification or IBM's Data Science Certificate, such credentials strengthen your application. Mention ongoing education and training to demonstrate your commitment to staying up to date with AI advancements. This signals professionalism, self-sufficiency, and alignment with current industry standards.

Using data to illustrate the impact of your AI expertise enhances your resume's appeal. Quantifiable achievements encapsulate your abilities effectively. If you've implemented AI solutions that led to significant sales growth or reduced processing time, include these statistics. They serve as tangible proof of your contributions and the value you bring to companies. If applying for roles focused on data analysis, consider incorporating visuals or graphs to highlight these results. A well-placed graph can instantly capture attention and convey information more effectively than words alone.

Visual Element: Checklist

Consider creating a checklist of AI projects, tools, certifications, and achievements you wish to showcase on your resume.

As we conclude this chapter, remember that an AI-ready resume exceeds being merely a skill inventory; it's a testament to navigating this pioneering field adeptly and assuredly. Assembling your resume, consider how each component—skills, experiences, education, and impact—conveys your unique AI journey. This comprehensive approach ensures you stand out in a crowded job market, showcasing not just accomplishments but future potential.

In the upcoming chapter, we'll explore AI's transformative potential beyond traditional technological confines, unlocking opportunities for innovation and evolution across a spectrum of industries. Stay tuned as we delve deeper into these thrilling possibilities awaiting exploration!

Chapter 9

Overcoming Challenges in AI Learning

Overcoming the Intimidation Factor: AI-Made Accessible

Imagine standing at the foot of a towering mountain, its peak cloaked in mist, symbolizing the intimidating challenge that learning AI presents. The path to mastering AI mirrors this daunting climb; however, it is a journey that can be traversed step by step, with perseverance and curiosity as companions. This ascent into the world of AI is not just an exploration of technology but also an exhilarating dive into creative problem-solving. Each component of AI is akin to a distinct piece of an intricate mosaic. By dissecting these pieces, a learner begins to see how each contributes to forming a cohesive, intelligent whole.

Demystifying AI starts with exploring its fundamental building blocks. Algorithms, for instance, serve as blueprints that direct computers to accomplish specific tasks, much like a detailed map. This analogy helps bridge the conceptual divide, as maps are familiar tools that guide us through unfamiliar territory. Similarly, understanding neural networks as interconnected neurons within a human brain transforms abstract concepts into tangible understanding. Picture this network as a bustling city where highways act as synapses transmitting signals, with regulators ensuring smooth traffic flow. Such visualizations make the intricate nature of AI more accessible and relatable.

Delve deeper into machine learning by likening it to a familiar scenario: teaching a child to recognize objects. Initially, a child might mistake a lion for a large dog—an understandable error given limited exposure. However, through gentle correction and continuous learning, they learn to differentiate the two. AI systems operate in much the same way, refining their understanding through iterative processes. This progression can also be compared to an artist sculpting a masterpiece from a block of marble—gradually, with precision, shaping raw data into meaningful insights.

Venturing into the vast landscape of AI requires the right educational resources. Platforms like Coursera and Khan Academy offer structured pathways that transform AI education into an engaging, manageable journey, breaking down complex topics into digestible lessons. Books like *AI for Dummies* serve as guiding lights, easing learners through the sometimes impenetrable fog of technical jargon. Building a solid foundation through well-chosen resources is akin to laying the groundwork for a skyscraper—each element contributes to the integrity of the whole structure.

Personal stories can serve as powerful motivators. Consider Jane, who transitioned from marketing management to AI analytics, demonstrating how openness to change and strategic learning can unlock AI's transformative potential. Similarly, Alex's entrepreneurial leap into streamlining supply chains with AI confirms that a technical background, while beneficial, isn't strictly necessary for AI proficiency. These stories illustrate that ambition, combined with the right opportunities, makes AI literacy accessible to all.

Moreover, cultivating a growth mindset is essential along this journey. AI leaders like Andrew Ng have faced and overcome initial hurdles, embodying the philosophy of lifelong learning. Viewing challenges as stepping stones rather than obstacles ensures continual progression. Ng's reflections emphasize that expertise stems from persistent effort and dedication, not innate talent. Insights from AI pioneers highlight that success in this field is built on resilience, adaptability, and tenacity.

Reflection Section: Your AI Path Forward

Pause and reflect on your personal aspirations within the AI landscape. What aspects of AI ignite your curiosity? Jot these thoughts down, as they will fuel your journey forward. Consider how your existing skills intertwine with AI concepts; perhaps your flair for storytelling can enhance user interface design, or an analytical mindset might lead you to excel in data interpretation. Recognizing and leveraging these strengths can make your AI exploration more fulfilling and enriching.

Empowering yourself with knowledge can transform AI from a perceived obstacle into a companion for growth in both personal and professional realms. By deconstructing complex ideas into understandable elements and employing relatable language, you transform AI into a familiar, approachable landscape rather than an unfathomable abyss. Engaging with beginner-friendly resources and learning from those who've successfully transitioned to AI makes the ascent toward understanding less formidable. With curiosity as your guide and perseverance by your side, the world of AI unfolds with clarity and confidence.

Avoiding Information Overload: Curating Your AI Learning Path

Imagine standing in an immense library, overwhelmed by endless rows of books on myriad topics. Such is the experience of learning AI, often presenting an abundance of information without clear guidance. The key to navigating this library is defining a focused learning path aligned with personal goals and motivations. Contemplate, "What do I aim to achieve with AI?" Whether it's optimizing business processes or revolutionizing healthcare, pinpointing your interests provides a sturdy framework for your knowledge journey, shielding you from the trap of information overload.

With your goals in place, choose resources tailored to your learning style and ambitions. Evaluate courses and workshops on platforms like edX and Coursera based on content quality and relevance. Opting for courses that deeply resonate with your aspirations ensures that each learning session adds value and understanding rather than becoming another digital detour.

Diversify the learning materials you use. Some individuals thrive on visual storytelling, such as videos or infographics, while others thrive on in-depth textual analysis or interactive sessions. Identify your preferred learning modes to enhance your educational experience's efficiency and enjoyment. Enrich your learning journey by embracing varied materials that address different aspects of AI.

Developing a structured learning plan serves as your roadmap through the AI landscape. Once you establish your learning preferences, translate them into a concrete plan, interweaving theory with hands-on practice. Allocate specific study times, punctuating them with practical exercises that cement theoretical concepts and boost confidence. This balanced approach ensures comprehension and engagement, transforming the learning process from overwhelming to enjoyable. A structured plan helps you navigate potential pitfalls and imbues your journey with a sense of direction and achievement as you tick off each milestone.

Regular reflection and reassessment of your learning plan allow for insightful refinement. Recognize when adjustments are needed—perhaps more focus on statistics or more profound exploration into a technical skill. Flexibility in approach maximizes productivity and retains motivation throughout your learning journey.

Integrating review sessions into your routine is quintessential for effective learning. Consistently revisiting and summarizing foundational concepts strengthens retention and reinforces understanding. Tools like flashcards or digital trackers can assist in monitoring progress and pinpointing areas needing attention. Engaging in continual review and reflection cultivates a profound and enduring connection with the material, unveiling deeper insights within your AI journey.

Engaging with AI Communities: Learning Together

Imagine being part of an energetic gathering where enthusiasts from diverse backgrounds share and expand their AI knowledge. Engaging with AI communities provides a collaborative environment for exchanging ideas, tackling challenges, and collectively exploring solutions. These communities offer a kaleidoscope of perspectives, enriching and enhancing your comprehension of AI concepts. By participating in online platforms like Reddit's r/MachineLearning or specialised groups on LinkedIn, you connect with a global network, gaining insights into diverse methodologies, staying informed about industry trends, and finding solidarity with peers pursuing similar paths.

AI events present invaluable networking opportunities and insights directly from industry pioneers. Whether attending hackathons, webinars, or meetups, these events serve as gateways to expanding your contacts and enriching your knowledge. Hackathons offer an immersive space to apply skills to real-world problems, while webinars expose you to cutting-edge expertise and innovations. Engaging with events immerses you in the vibrant AI ecosystem, sparking inspiration and fuelling academic pursuits.

Collaborative projects further enhance practical learning and teamwork skills. Whether contributing to initiatives on platforms like GitHub or joining virtual study groups, these collaborations foster creativity and deepen your understanding of AI. Working alongside others bridges the gap between theoretical learning and practical application, helping you apply knowledge in real-world contexts.

Group activities foster essential soft skills critical to careers involving AI. These experiences cultivate collaboration, effective communication, and leadership qualities, adding invaluable dimensions to your skill set. By participating in forums where diverse ideas meet, you catalyse potential innovation and breakthroughs.

Staying Updated: Tools and Resources for Continuous Learning

Remaining abreast of AI's advancements is vital in this fast-evolving field. Regularly exploring platforms that update on AI innovations, such as newsletters like AI Weekly or specialized AI podcasts, equips you with continuous awareness of technological progression. Embedding proactive learning into your schedule fosters adaptability and prepares you for emerging challenges and opportunities.

Allocate periods for skill enhancement through new AI topics, broadening your understanding and positioning you at the vanguard of innovation. Platforms like edX and Coursera offer advanced coursework as part of this ongoing educational journey. Additionally, pursuing professional certification not only affirms your skillset but elevates career opportunities within the industry.

Follow influential AI researchers and thought leaders on platforms like Twitter or LinkedIn for deeper exploration. Their insights and shared expertise add a nuanced layer of understanding and update you on the latest AI trends and breakthroughs.

Embracing Mistakes: Learning and Growing with AI

Mistakes should not be considered failures but essential components of the learning curve in the pursuit of mastering AI. Each error harbors potential insights leading to mastery. Early setbacks recounted by AI experts illustrate how such experiences often pave the way to triumphs. Reflecting on and learning from mistakes yields awareness and encourages better-crafted problem-solving strategies.

To overcome challenges effectively, utilize problem-solving methodologies like root cause analysis and iterative testing. These techniques help identify faults within AI models and refine solutions over time. Reflective practices encourage evolution, nurture critical thinking, and strengthen acumen.

Innovation often flourishes when results deviate from expectations; a narrative echoed in AI project case studies where initial setbacks led to successful alternative paths. Embrace the spirit of experimentation, viewing mistakes as fertile ground for creativity and learning and transforming anomalies into avenues for exploration.

This mindset involves meticulous documentation and analysis of challenges, maintaining a comprehensive record of obstacles and solutions implemented. Such a log becomes a valuable resource for future endeavors, ensuring continuous learning through past experiences, saving effort, and preventing repeated missteps.

Mistakes foster a creative and conducive learning environment. Encouraging experimentation, embracing failures, and iterating builds monumental achievements rooted in initial setbacks. By accepting mistakes as part of your evolution, you advance not only in your AI journey but also in personal growth, navigating barriers with increased agility and insight. With each challenge, you forge a path toward success equipped with the wisdom gained from adapting and overcoming.

Chapter 10

Realizing the Potential of AI

Case Studies: AI Success Stories Across Industries

Imagine a world where your visit to a doctor is as efficient as the click of a button. You walk in, and even before you sit down, the results are ready, thanks to an AI system that has scoured thousands of medical reports to provide the most accurate diagnosis. This isn't a futuristic dream—it's the reality AI is crafting in healthcare today. Artificial intelligence is revolutionising diagnostics and patient care by sifting through mountains of data with unparalleled speed and precision. Companies like IBM Watson Health have developed AI systems that assist doctors in diagnosing diseases earlier and more accurately by analysing medical images and records, leading to better patient outcomes and cost savings for healthcare systems.

Yet, the reach of AI in healthcare extends beyond mere diagnostics. Imagine, if you will, that AI is infusing the entire spectrum of patient interaction, transforming treatment plans into living documents. These dynamic plans adjust in real-time, taking into account new data about genetic expressions, lifestyle choices, and even shifts in environmental factors. This personalised medicine is more than just a trend—it's a leap towards treatments that are uniquely tailored, held together by the intricate mesh of each individual's life circumstances. Furthermore, AI tools that can predict potential side effects and suggest alternative medications offer newfound layers of safety and efficacy, providing a robust safety net for patients navigating complex treatments. The ripple effect of these developments can be observed in patients' improved quality of life and the gradual reduction in hospital readmissions.

To further illustrate the profound impact of AI in healthcare, consider its application in surgery. Robotic surgery systems powered by AI enhance a surgeon's precision through improved imaging and analysis, leading to minimally invasive procedures with faster recovery times. As AI continues to evolve, these systems will likely handle even more complex surgical tasks, providing tangible benefits to both clinicians and patients. AI's role in telemedicine also cannot be overlooked; platforms that support remote consultations have become indispensable, especially during unprecedented times such as global health crises. These innovations facilitate contactless healthcare services, enabling patients to receive medical attention without needing to travel, thereby widening access to healthcare services across geographical and socio-economic boundaries.

In the financial realm, AI is redefining the very concept of trust and security. Envision a vigilant guard that never sleeps, tirelessly monitoring transactions for any signs of fraudulent activity. Financial institutions leverage AI algorithms to detect unusual patterns in real-time, preventing billions in losses. Companies like Mastercard employ AI-driven tools that scan millions of transactions per second, identifying potential fraud before it impacts customers. These systems not only bolster individual account security but also enhance trust in financial services by providing an additional layer of protection. Moreover, AI is weaving itself into the fabric of finance, optimising trading strategies by analysing historical and real-time data to predict market movements. This enables traders to make more informed decisions, minimising risks and maximising returns. Furthermore, AI in finance is about protection, prediction, and personalisation. For instance, the rise of robo-advisors powered by AI offers personalised investment recommendations by analysing a client's financial goals and risk tolerance, democratising access to investment advice by making it available to a broader audience. This approach facilitates informed financial decisions, catering to investors from diverse backgrounds, thereby levelling the playing field in a previously exclusivist industry. Additionally, AI-driven credit scoring models provide fairer assessments by considering a variety of non-traditional data sources, aiming for more inclusive lending practices and opening financial opportunities for those previously underserved.

Often perceived as traditional, agriculture is undergoing a technological renaissance courtesy of AI. Picture a farmer using a smartphone to check soil conditions, forecast weather patterns, and manage crop health—all from a device in their palm. AI is improving crop yield through precision farming techniques that optimise resources and reduce waste. By analysing data from drones and sensors, farmers can make informed decisions about watering schedules and pesticide application, ensuring healthier crops and sustainable practices. These advancements not only boost productivity but also contribute to global food security. Imagine autonomous tractors guided by AI, ploughing fields with precision, significantly reducing human labour and enhancing efficiency.

Further enriching this agricultural tapestry, AI aids in crop disease management. Machine learning algorithms can detect early signs of plant diseases, allowing for proactive interventions before an outbreak devastates the crops. This early intervention approach is crucial for maintaining yields and reducing economic losses, supporting small-scale farmers who are heavily reliant on crop success. The combination of real-time data processing and predictive analytics empowers farmers, making agriculture a proactive rather than reactive endeavour and fostering environments where both nature and technology thrive symbiotically.

AI's utility in agriculture extends to animal husbandry. Imagine AI systems monitoring livestock health through wearable sensors that track vital statistics, detecting potential illnesses before they become widespread. This preemptive care ensures healthier livestock, leading to higher-quality produce and increased farmer profitability. AI's role in sustainable agriculture also supports efforts to tackle climate change by optimising inputs and reducing greenhouse gas emissions.

The success stories across these industries share common threads: cross-functional collaboration, continuous optimisation, and visionary leadership. In healthcare, collaboration between AI teams and medical professionals has been crucial. Doctors work alongside data scientists to refine algorithms, ensuring they align with clinical practices. Continuous monitoring of AI models allows for ongoing improvements and adaptation to new medical research, maintaining accuracy and relevance. These efforts represent a harmonious fusion of medical expertise and technological innovation, creating outcomes that neither field could achieve alone.

Strong leadership has been essential in integrating AI into existing frameworks. In finance, leaders who embrace innovation drive the adoption of AI tools, fostering a culture of agility and openness to change. They establish clear objectives for AI initiatives and guide teams towards successful implementation. Moreover, continuous optimisation ensures AI systems remain effective as threats evolve. This perpetual cycle of feedback and refinement keeps financial institutions agile and responsive to emerging risks and opportunities.

Challenges such as data quality and organisational resistance often arise during AI implementation. In agriculture, ensuring the availability of high-quality data from diverse sources is paramount. Farmers must integrate data from various technologies, such as satellite imagery and sensor networks, to create comprehensive insights. Addressing resistance to change requires clear communication of AI's benefits and training programmes that empower stakeholders. By demystifying AI and illustrating its tangible benefits, leaders can foster trust and enthusiasm among users.

Lessons learned from these case studies emphasise the importance of setting clear objectives and leveraging user feedback. In healthcare, defining specific goals, such as reducing diagnostic errors, guides AI development efforts. User feedback loops allow continuous refinement based on real-world experiences, resulting in more robust systems. These systems are not static; they evolve through continual feedback and improvement, enhancing their efficacy and relevance in transforming industries and improving lives.

These stories are not just about technology—they're about transformation. They demonstrate how AI can bridge gaps between industries, enhance capabilities, and create new opportunities. The journey towards realising AI's potential involves embracing challenges as opportunities for growth. It's about harnessing the power of collaboration, innovation, and leadership to shape a future where AI enhances human lives. It acts as a catalyst for accelerating positive change across multiple facets of society.

Interactive Element: Reflecting on AI's Impact

Consider how AI technologies might transform your industry or personal projects. Reflect on potential applications, challenges, and ways to collaborate with others to ensure successful implementation. Engaging in this reflective practice illuminates AI's potential within your context and clarifies how you can effectively harness its power.

Each case study offers a roadmap for your own AI initiatives. By understanding the strategies that led to success, you can apply best practices tailored to your unique needs and goals. Whether you're in healthcare, finance, or any other field, the key lies in fostering collaboration and maintaining a commitment to continuous improvement. As you explore the possibilities of AI in your context, remember that its true potential lies in its ability to transform industries and lives alike. It can be a beacon, guiding us towards more efficient, innovative, and inclusive futures.

In healthcare, imagine designing an AI system that predicts patient outcomes based on genetic data or lifestyle factors. Collaborate with medical experts to integrate insights seamlessly into patient care plans. In finance, envision developing an AI tool that enhances customer experience by providing personalised financial advice while maintaining security standards. These integrated approaches signify a burgeoning era of personalised and secure services across diverse sectors.

Agriculture offers opportunities for sustainable practices through AI-driven resource management. Imagine using drones equipped with AI capabilities to monitor crop health from above, identifying areas needing attention before issues arise. This would maximise resources, reduce waste, and set the stage for a more sustainable and secure global food supply.

By learning from these examples, you gain valuable insights into overcoming challenges such as data integration or organisational resistance. Set clear objectives aligned with broader goals while remaining adaptable to changing circumstances. These practices ensure that AI deployments stay relevant and impactful.

Continuous improvement is vital; leverage user feedback through surveys or focus groups to refine solutions iteratively. Embrace user-centric design principles when developing interfaces or features—ensuring accessibility enhances adoption rates among diverse users. When people from different backgrounds comfortably engage with AI systems, the potential for creating equitable solutions drastically increases.

The journey to realising AI's potential involves embracing collaboration across disciplines—bridging gaps between technology developers and domain experts fosters innovation at every stage. Strong leadership guides teams through transitions smoothly while promoting a culture open to experimentation. Encouraging open dialogue and sharing success stories within the field cultivates an environment where innovation thrives.

As you embark on your own path towards leveraging AI's transformative power within your industry or personal pursuits, draw inspiration from these success stories. The lessons learned along their respective paths provide invaluable guidance for your endeavours ahead. Adopting a strategic yet flexible approach to AI becomes a cornerstone for fostering environments ripe with potential and progress.

The Human-AI Collaboration: Enhancing Creativity and Innovation

Imagine sitting at your desk with a blank canvas before you, ready to create. Now, picture an AI tool as your sidekick, nudging you with suggestions, enhancing your ideas, and pointing out patterns you might not have noticed. This synergy between human creativity and AI's analytical prowess is reshaping how we innovate and solve problems. AI is not just a tool; it's an amplifier of human ingenuity. It helps you explore new possibilities by swiftly processing vast amounts of data, offering insights that could take you hours, if not days, to decipher on your own. It's like having a brainstorming buddy who never tires and always has fresh ideas.

In the art world, this collaboration is breaking new ground. Artists are using AI to push boundaries and generate entirely new art forms.

Consider how AI algorithms assist artists in creating intricate visual patterns or even composing music. Musicians are merging traditional techniques with AI-generated soundscapes, resulting in tracks that blend human emotion with machine precision. This partnership allows for the exploration of sound in ways previously unimaginable, crafting unique auditory experiences that resonate on multiple levels. These intersections of technology and creativity broaden the horizons of artistry, providing artists with novel pathways to express and evolve their craft.

AI's impact on art extends to curation as well. Museums use AI to analyse visitor preferences, helping curators design exhibits that engage audiences more effectively. AI-driven insights into art appreciation patterns allow curators to create experiences that resonate on a more personal level, increasing visitor engagement and satisfaction. By customizing art displays to fit visitor interests, museums provide enriching, tailored experiences to their audiences, expanding the influence of art in society.

Fashion designers are also embracing AI to innovate clothing patterns. Imagine a designer feeding their sketches into an AI system, offering multiple variations, suggesting colours and patterns that might not have been considered otherwise. It's like having a digital muse encouraging experimentation and risk-taking in a field where creativity is paramount. These collaborations do not replace the human element but enhance it, allowing designers to focus on their vision while AI handles the technical intricacies. AI drives innovation in the design realm, prompting designers to transcend traditional limits and aim for new pinnacles of creativity.

AI is revolutionizing design processes in architecture. Architects can use AI to simulate the environmental impacts of their plans, ensuring sustainable designs that adapt to climate challenges. AI tools can optimize material usage and structural stability, leading to innovative buildings that balance aesthetics with functionality. This fusion of technology and design promotes environmentally sensitive building practices while preserving architectural creativity and flair.

However, as we integrate AI into creative processes, ethical considerations become more important. Transparency is crucial when AI generates content. Consumers have the right to know what role AI plays in the creation process. This transparency ensures that while AI assists in the creative process, the work's authenticity remains intact. For example, in music or art, where AI contributes significantly, acknowledging its role respects both the human creator and the technology involved.

Preserving authenticity is another vital aspect. The human touch must remain evident even as AI contributes to art or design. The final decision-making should rest with humans to ensure the output genuinely reflects their vision and emotions. This balance maintains creativity's essence while leveraging AI's capabilities. Retaining human essence in creations reaffirms the intrinsic value of human intuition, feeling, and originality.

Embracing collaboration with AI involves more than just adopting new tools; it requires a shift in mindset toward experimentation and innovation. Think about areas in your projects where AI can add value. Perhaps you're working on a personal project or professional task where data analysis could be enhanced through AI tools. These tools can streamline workflows, improve efficiency, and save time for more strategic thinking. The integration of AI acts as a catalyst for creative breakthroughs, blending technology with human intuition for a richer tapestry of innovation.

Collaborating with AI tools doesn't mean relinquishing control; instead, it means augmenting your capabilities. For instance, if you're involved in content creation, AI can help generate initial drafts or suggest edits based on readability and engagement metrics. This collaboration allows you to focus on refining ideas and crafting compelling narratives without getting bogged down by routine tasks. It streamlines mundane processes, granting creators more freedom to perfect the substance and style of their work.

Identifying opportunities for collaboration begins with recognizing repetitive tasks or areas where additional insights could be valuable. Explore available AI tools that align with your goals and experiment with integrating them into your workflow. The key is to view AI as an ally that supports your creative pursuits while offering new perspectives. In this synergy, the sum of AI and human ingenuity exceeds their individual contributions, heralding a new era of creativity.

Imagine leveraging AI for brainstorming sessions. Picture an AI-powered tool that analyses current trends in your field and suggests innovative ideas based on data patterns it detects. You can then build upon these suggestions, incorporating your unique insights to create something truly original. This process enhances creativity and empowers you to tackle challenges more effectively. The iterative process, fueled by AI's analytical prowess and human ingenuity, leads to groundbreaking innovations and solutions.

AI's potential extends beyond individual projects and fosters collaborative efforts across teams and disciplines. Consider how AI might facilitate communication between departments by providing shared platforms for data analysis or project management. This integration promotes transparency and efficiency across organizations while encouraging diverse perspectives. Fostering a collaborative environment where AI enhances dialogue leads to unparalleled symbiotic achievements.

As we continue exploring human-AI collaboration, it's important to remember that this partnership should enhance rather than replace human ingenuity. By maintaining control over decision-making processes and ensuring transparency in AI's contributions, we can strike a balance that respects both human creativity and technological advancements. The harmonious coexistence of human intelligence and artificial intelligence heralds a future brimming with possibilities, where the innovation potential is boundless.

In music composition, imagine collaborating with an AI tool capable of generating melodies based on existing tracks' emotional tone or tempo. This tool would serve as a creative partner rather than a replacement for musical talent, offering new directions while preserving artistic intent. Musicians would harness AI's augmented creativity, leading to harmonious works that encapsulate the nuances of human emotion and technological precision.

Similarly, fashion designers can use AI-generated patterns as inspiration rather than definitive designs—allowing them to interpret suggestions through their own unique style lenses before finalizing pieces. This distinct collaboration fuels a world of infinite styles and trends, enriching the fashion landscape with diversity and uniqueness.

The ethical implications of such collaborations extend beyond transparency. They encompass issues related to authorship rights when machines play significant roles alongside humans within creative processes. Addressing these concerns requires ongoing discourse among creators about how best practices might evolve alongside technological advancements to ensure equitable recognition across all contributors involved in collaborative projects involving artificial intelligence applications today. Striking a fair balance fosters ethical, inclusive environments where human and AI contributions are recognized.

In conclusion (without summarizing), embracing collaboration with artificial intelligence opens doors toward enhanced innovation through augmented creativity across diverse fields—from arts and design sectors right down into everyday personal endeavors, too! As this collaboration strengthens, the line between art and science blurs, creating new experiences and redefining the boundaries of creativity. The potential for human-AI collaboration transcends current limitations, presenting endless opportunities to reinvent the narratives of technology-infused human creativity.

Envisioning the Future: Your Role in the AI Revolution

Let's talk about your role in this AI revolution. It's easy to think of AI as happening in tech labs or corporate boardrooms, but people like you are shaping AI's future. Yes, you have the power to drive positive change. Imagine joining AI advocacy groups or initiatives where you can voice your opinions, concerns, and ideas. These groups are often platforms for lively discussions on AI ethics and policy, two areas where diverse perspectives are needed to ensure that the technology serves everyone reasonably. By getting involved, you're not just observing the change but part of it. This proactive engagement can start small—maybe a local meetup or an online forum—but can grow into something more impactful over time.

Keeping pace with AI's rapid evolution means embracing lifelong learning and being ready to adapt. One way to do this is by pursuing advanced AI courses and certifications. These programs don't just expand your knowledge; they also enhance your credibility in the field. Think of them as stepping stones, helping you stay relevant as the industry evolves. Engaging with thought leaders and AI communities is another strategy. Platforms like LinkedIn offer access to professionals who are at the forefront of developing new AI technologies. You can gain insights into emerging trends and innovations by following them, participating in discussions, or attending webinars.

AI's societal impact is broad and deep, touching everything from healthcare to finance to environmental sustainability. For example, AI holds great potential in addressing global challenges like climate change. Imagine AI systems that can analyse vast amounts of ecological data to predict weather patterns or optimize energy use. These applications help mitigate climate impacts and promote sustainable practices that benefit communities worldwide. Your role here can be as an advocate for these solutions, pushing for their adoption and refinement.

Inclusivity and diversity in AI development are crucial for ensuring equitable benefits. Diverse teams bring varied perspectives, leading to more innovative solutions that reflect the needs of different communities. You can promote inclusivity by supporting initiatives encouraging underrepresented groups to enter AI or advocating for diverse hiring practices within organizations. Inclusion fosters environments that breed creativity and innovation, unlocking AI's full potential to deliver on its promise across all of society's strata.

Becoming a leader in the AI field isn't reserved for those with technical backgrounds alone. It's about driving innovation and ethical practices that prioritize human values. Mentoring the next generation of AI professionals is one way to inspire future leaders. By sharing your experiences and knowledge, you help cultivate a culture of learning and curiosity. This mentorship can take many forms—from formal programs to informal guidance through online platforms.

Leading initiatives for responsible AI deployment involves setting standards for ethical use and ensuring that AI systems are transparent and accountable. As a leader, you can shape how AI is used within your organization or community, promoting practices that align with societal values and ethical principles. Responsible leadership creates a backbone for trustworthy AI, instilling public confidence in AI's potential to drive progress and solve complex challenges.

The path to realizing AI's full potential lies in active engagement, continuous learning, and a commitment to inclusivity and ethical leadership. These elements are not isolated; they work together to create a future where AI serves as a tool for positive change across all sectors of society. Championing open and chronicled pathways for AI's deployment merges ethical well-being with technological prowess.

As we wrap up this chapter, let's reflect on the bigger picture. The AI revolution is not just about technology; it's about people coming together to shape a better future. Each of us has a role to play, whether it's advocating for ethical practices, driving innovation, or inspiring others through mentorship and leadership. The next chapter will delve into how these principles apply across different industries, exploring real-world applications that demonstrate the transformative power of AI when guided by human insight and compassion. Let's continue this journey towards an AI-driven world that reflects our shared aspirations and values. The triumph lies in weaving technology into the human tapestry, creating a design rich with dreams, shared responsibilities, and optimism for tomorrow.

Conclusion

As we come to the end of our journey together, let's take a moment to reflect on the path we've traveled. We've explored the vast landscape of artificial intelligence, starting with its foundational concepts. You learned about how AI mimics human intelligence and discovered the fascinating world of machine learning, where computers learn from data to make informed decisions. From there, we delved into the practical applications of AI in business, showcasing how AI-driven tools can revolutionize marketing, customer service, and operations. We also navigated the ethical considerations that arise as AI becomes an integral part of our lives, emphasizing the importance of responsible implementation.

The vision behind this book was to demystify AI for non-technical professionals and students like you. My goal was to make AI accessible and practical, empowering you with the knowledge and strategies to leverage AI for enhanced productivity in your personal and professional life. Whether seeking to optimize business operations or simply curious about AI's impact on the future, this book provides a solid foundation.

As you reflect on the pages you've turned, several key takeaways emerge. First, ethical AI practices are paramount. As AI continues transforming industries, ensuring fairness, transparency, and accountability in its application is crucial. Second, the dynamics between human creativity and AI innovation presents a unique opportunity. AI can augment our capabilities, helping us solve complex problems and unlock new possibilities. Finally, understanding AI's impact on the workforce and society prepares you for future changes. By embracing AI with an open mind, you can harness its potential to drive positive change.

But the journey doesn't end here. I encourage you to continue exploring the world of AI. Dive deeper into advanced topics, engage with AI communities, and stay updated on emerging trends. Platforms like Coursera, edX, and AI-focused forums offer countless resources to fuel your curiosity. By continuing your education, you can stay at the forefront of AI advancements and further enhance your skills.

Now, it's time to take action. Apply what you've learned to your daily life. Start with small AI projects that pique your interest. Experiment with AI tools in your workplace or explore how AI can streamline your personal tasks. Join community discussions to share your insights and advocate for responsible AI practices. Your involvement is crucial in shaping the future of AI. Each step you take contributes to a more significant movement toward ethical and impactful AI integration.

You are uniquely positioned in the AI revolution, and your voice matters. Participating actively can help address challenges and ensure AI serves humanity positively. As you embark on this path, remember that you're not alone. I'm grateful for the opportunity to share this journey with you. Your insights and feedback are invaluable as we continue to learn and grow together. I invite you to connect and share your experiences—let's build a community of AI enthusiasts committed to making a difference.

In closing, I want to leave you with an inspiring thought. AI is a powerful tool with the potential to transform our world for the better. Embrace it with curiosity and a commitment to ethical applications. Together, we can drive innovation and create a future where AI uplifts society. Thank you for joining me on this adventure. I look forward to seeing the incredible ways you will harness AI's potential to create meaningful change.

Keeping the Knowledge Alive

Now you have everything you need to understand and use AI confidently, it's time to share what you've learned and show other readers where they can find the same helpful guidance.

By leaving your honest opinion of this book on Amazon, you'll help other beginners and non-technical professionals find the information they're looking for and pass on the excitement of learning about artificial intelligence.

Thank you for helping spread the power of AI—your support ensures the knowledge keeps growing.

https://www.amazon.com/dp/B0F59SQ3R8

References

1. Timeline of artificial intelligence. (n.d.). In Wikipedia. Retrieved March 24, 2025, from https://en.wikipedia.org/wiki/Timeline_of_artificial_intelligence
2. IBM. (n.d.). Understanding the different types of artificial intelligence. Retrieved March 24, 2025, from https://www.ibm.com/think/topics/artificial-intelligence-types
3. Alderman, H. (2024, March 1). AI will have a significant impact on labor markets. Here's how ... FedScoop. Retrieved from https://fedscoop.com/ai-will-have-a-major-impact-on-labor-markets-heres-how-the-us-can-prepare/
4. Bipartisan Policy Center. (n.d.). AI: Facts and myths. Retrieved March 24, 2025, from https://bipartisanpolicy.org/explainer/ai-facts-and-myths/
5. GeeksforGeeks. (n.d.). Machine learning tutorial. Retrieved March 24, 2025, from https://www.geeksforgeeks.org/machine-learning/
6. Google Cloud. (n.d.). Supervised vs. unsupervised learning. Retrieved March 24, 2025, from https://cloud.google.com/discover/supervised-vs-unsupervised-learning#:~:text=The%20biggest%20difference%20between%20supervised,correct%20output%20values%20should%20be.
7. Number Analytics. (n.d.). Practical decision trees: Real-world examples and implementation tips. Retrieved March 24, 2025, from https://www.numberanalytics.com/blog/practical-decision-trees-real-world-examples-implementation-tips
8. ResearchGate. (n.d.). What are the challenges associated with training deep neural networks? Retrieved March 24, 2025, from https://www.researchgate.net/post/What_are_the_challenges_associated_with_training_deep_neural_networks
9. IBM. (n.d.). AI in marketing. Retrieved March 24, 2025, from https://www.ibm.com/think/topics/ai-in-marketing

10. DataRails. (n.d.). Top 6 predictive analytics tools, techniques, and examples. Retrieved March 24, 2025, from https://www.datarails.com/top-predictive-analytics-tools/
11. FEPBL. (2023). AI-driven financial forecasting: Innovations. International Journal of Applied Economics. Retrieved March 24, 2025, from https://www.fepbl.com/index.php/ijae/article/view/1231
12. Gartner. (n.d.). AI roadmap: What it is and how to build one. Retrieved March 24, 2025, from https://www.gartner.com/en/articles/ai-roadmap
13. Gearbrain. (n.d.). AI in smart homes: Security, efficiency & automation. Retrieved March 24, 2025, from https://www.gearbrain.com/ai-smart-home-automation-devices-2671168897.html
14. Google Research. (2023). Advancing personal health and wellness insights with AI. Retrieved March 24, 2025, from https://research.google/blog/advancing-personal-health-and-wellness-insights-with-ai/
15. Forbes. (2024, July 22). Personalised learning and AI: Revolutionizing education. Retrieved from https://www.forbes.com/councils/forbestechcouncil/2024/07/22/personalised-learning-and-ai-revolutionizing-education/
16. AppInventiv. (n.d.). AI in travel and tourism – 10 benefits, use cases and examples. Retrieved March 24, 2025, from https://appinventiv.com/blog/ai-in-travel/#:~:text=and%20their%20impact.-,Improved%20Travel%20Safety%20and%20Security,activities%20using%20real%2Dtime%20monitoring.
17. DataCamp. (n.d.). Exploring 12 of the best data visualization tools in 2023. Retrieved March 24, 2025, from https://www.datacamp.com/blog/12-of-the-best-data-visualizations-tools
18. ICD10Monitor. (n.d.). Understanding business intelligence and the impact of AI. Retrieved March 24, 2025, from https://icd10monitor.medlearn.com/understanding-business-intelligence-and-the-impact-of-ai/
19. Cypher Learning. (2024). Infographic: 8 predictions for AI in 2024. Retrieved March 24, 2025, from

https://www.cypherlearning.com/resources/infographics/predictions-for-ai-in-2024

20. Microsoft. (n.d.). AI for beginners. Retrieved March 24, 2025, from https://microsoft.github.io/AI-For-Beginners/
21. Securiti.ai. (n.d.). The impact of the GDPR on artificial intelligence. Retrieved March 24, 2025, from https://securiti.ai/impact-of-the-gdpr-on-artificial-intelligence/
22. Datatron. (n.d.). Real-life examples of discriminating artificial intelligence. Retrieved March 24, 2025, from https://datatron.com/real-life-examples-of-discriminating-artificial-intelligence/
23. Harvard Business Review. (2022, July). Why you need an AI ethics committee. Retrieved from https://hbr.org/2022/07/why-you-need-an-ai-ethics-committee#:~:text=The%20Function%20and%20Jurisdiction%20of%20an%20AI%20Ethics%20Committee&text=At%20a%20high%20level%20the,purchased%20from%20third%2Dparty%20vendors.
24. Princeton University. (n.d.). Case studies - Princeton dialogues on AI and ethics. Retrieved March 24, 2025, from https://aiethics.princeton.edu/case-studies/
25. Jellyfish Technologies. (n.d.). AI and IoT convergence: Benefits and real-world examples. Retrieved March 24, 2025, from https://www.jellyfishtechnologies.com/convergence-of-ai-and-iot/
26. Fortune Business Insights. (2023). Cloud AI market size, share & growth analysis report [2030]. Retrieved March 24, 2025, from https://www.fortunebusinessinsights.com/cloud-ai-market-108878
27. eSecurity Planet. (n.d.). AI and cyber security: Innovations and challenges. Retrieved March 24, 2025, from https://www.esecurityplanet.com/trends/ai-and-cybersecurity-innovations-and-challenges/
28. Mdpi. (2023). Autonomous vehicles: Evolution of artificial intelligence. Retrieved March 24, 2025, from https://www.mdpi.com/2504-2289/8/4/42
29. Multiverse. (2024). The top skills you need for AI jobs in 2024. Retrieved March 24, 2025, from https://www.multiverse.io/en-US/blog/top-ai-skills
30. VKTR. (n.d.). 10 top AI certifications for non-technical professionals. Retrieved March 24, 2025, from https://www.vktr.com/ai-upskilling/10-top-ai-certifications-for-pros-without-technical-backgrounds/

31. Join the Collective. (n.d.). AI in mentorship: Enhancing human connections for. Retrieved March 24, 2025, from https://www.jointhecollective.com/article/mentorship-in-the-age-of-ai/
32. Buffer. (n.d.). 8 of the best AI productivity tools to help you optimize. Retrieved March 24, 2025, from https://buffer.com/resources/ai-productivity-tools/
33. Asana Forum. (2023). A non-technical enthusiast's journey to working on AI full-time: Lessons from helping to build Asana's AI strategy. Retrieved March 24, 2025, from https://forum.asana.com/t/a-non-technical-enthusiasts-journey-to-working-on-ai-full-time-lessons-from-helping-to-build-asanas-ai-strategy/983745
34. Quora. (n.d.). What are the best online discussion forums on artificial intelligence? Retrieved March 24, 2025, from https://www.quora.com/What-are-the-best-online-discussion-forums-on-artificial-intelligence
35. McKinsey & Company. (2023). The state of AI in 2023: Generative AI's breakout year. Retrieved March 24, 2025, from https://www.mckinsey.com/capabilities/quantumblack/our-insights/the-state-of-ai-in-2023-generative-ais-breakout-year
36. DJ Holt Law. (n.d.). AI in healthcare: Early success stories and lessons learned from leading health systems. Retrieved March 24, 2025, from https://djholtlaw.com/ai-in-healthcare-early-success-stories-and-lessons-learned-from-leading-health-systems/
37. Medium. (n.d.). Creative collaboration: How artists and AI can work together. Retrieved March 24, 2025, from https://medium.com/higher-neurons/creative-collaboration-how-artists-and-ai-can-work-together-187502fd8fdb
38. UNESCO. (n.d.). Ethics of artificial intelligence. Retrieved March 24, 2025, from https://www.unesco.org/en/artificial-intelligence/recommendation-ethics
39. Built In. (n.d.). The future of AI: How AI is changing the world. Retrieved March 24, 2025, from https://builtin.com/artificial-intelligence/artificial-intelligence-future#:~:text=What%20does%20the%20future%20of,and%20worries%20over%20job%20losses.

Printed in Dunstable, United Kingdom